GRILLING WITH
HOUSE OF Q

BBQ BRIAN MISKO

GRILLING WITH
HOUSE
OF Q

INSPIRED
RECIPES FOR
BACKYARD
BARBECUES

Figure 1
Vancouver / Berkeley

Cataloguing data available from Library and Archives Canada

ISBN 978-1-927958-10-0 (pbk.)

Editing by Lucy Kenward
Copy editing by Grace Yaginuma
Cover and interior design by Naomi MacDougall
Cover and interior photographs by Kevin Clark, except pages 3
and 42 (bottom) which are courtesy of the author
Printed and bound in China by C&C Offset Printing Co., Ltd.
Distributed in the U.S. by Publishers Group West

Figure 1 Publishing Inc.
Vancouver, BC Canada
www.figure1pub.com

CONTENTS

A WORD OF
WELCOME

Grilling with House of Q is a collection of recipes and stories that I have gathered as I've chosen to make competition BBQ, grilling and smoking my occupation. I didn't go to culinary school nor did I apprentice with the world's best restaurant chefs. I learned gradually, reading for hours and crafting many, many meals on a grill for years as my weekend hobby slowly took over my life. Even though a formal culinary education wasn't in the cards, that hasn't stopped me from winning the hearts of plenty of trained competition-BBQ critics (a.k.a. judges). I've collected a roomful of trophies and ribbons from many barbecue competitions, both nearby and across North America. The trophies are tokens of celebration, but more rewarding are the eight years of sharing my best barbecue tips with thousands of home cooks through numerous TV appearances and radio shows, at trade shows and through articles in magazines and newspapers. Ultimately I know that many people can learn from my adventures and experience so they can win the hearts of their own barbecue judges, their own family and friends. This book gathers the best of the tips, lessons and inspiring recipes.

Barbecue is not about cooking for one or two people—it's about cooking for a group and sharing a meal. You see, when planning a meal, it is just as easy to cook two racks of ribs as it is to cook one. And while you are doing the ribs, why not cook up some Mac 'n' Cheese (page 143) or put together a Grilled Corn, Black Bean and Peach Salad (page 138) or bake some of Brian's Cornbread (page 140)? It is just as easy to cook a couple of dishes for six or eight people as it is to cook for two. Just remember to invite some guests.

I want to inspire novice cooks to be brave and to try cooking on the grill. I want to show those who know their way around a grill how to play: to see new ideas, to expand on their skills or to round out a meal with appetizers, side dishes and desserts. So please, be creative, be confident and make a delicious dish. Your dinner guests are waiting.

———

With smoky BBQ goodness and love,
BBQ Brian

INTRODUCTION

I LIKE STORIES. I LIKE SEEING LIFE AS AN ADVENTURE AND KNOWING IT IS A SERIES OF STORIES, EACH NEW ONE FOLLOWED BY ANOTHER. I'VE GOT LOTS OF STORIES TO SHARE ABOUT MY EXPLOITS AS A COMPETITION-BBQ PITMASTER AND AS A TEACHER OF BACKYARD BARBECUE COOKS. AND IT ALL STARTS WITH A STORY ABOUT A SHORT DAY TRIP. . .

DUDE, WE'RE DOING THIS!

For a number of years, I worked as a sales representative for a software company and often had the opportunity to travel from my home in Canada to different regions of the United States. On those trips, I visited a lot of local restaurants, and, ultimately, I came across real Southern-style, slow-smoked barbecue. I don't recall a specific restaurant that I went to, but I do know that what I was experiencing was very different from anything I had ever experienced on an outdoor grill. The flavours were captivating, and I started to seek out more information about this beautiful and enticing cuisine. I wanted to know how it was cooked, how it was prepared, and through that process I learned there were *barbecue competitions*.

When I returned home, I found—much to my surprise—that a local barbecue competition was coming up. I asked my friend Glenn Erho if we could take our wives on a short day trip to see it. I wanted to know if it was like what I had experienced in the Southern states.

We made the two-hour trip to the event and met team after team of pitmasters who were more than willing to chat about what they were doing and how the contest worked. I felt like we were two boys seeing our favourite sports stars for the first time and soaking up every tidbit of information we could take in. We asked questions, lots of them, but the best part was going from tent to tent to sample the food after the teams had submitted their entries to the judges.

We started with pulled pork that was tender, tasty and some of the most intensely flavourful I have ever experienced. We met Myron Mixon of Jack's Old South, who is the "winningest" man in competition BBQ. Memorably, he allowed us to sample his brisket. It was simply divine. We watched Paul Kirk, the Kansas City Baron of Barbecue and a multiple World Barbecue Champion, glaze his ribs. They were smoky, sweet and just about good enough to eat both the meat and the bone! Later, at the awards ceremony, we witnessed Ron Shewchuk—who is now our friend, mentor and "key influencer" in getting us cooking—beat every other team and win the top prize. His was the first Canadian team to win the Grand Championship, and the whole experience was amazing. It seemed that afternoon like we filled our heads with knowledge and ate our body weight in barbecue samples. And we loved it.

On the way home, with a smile on my face and my imagination still reeling from our experience, I turned to Glenn and declared, "Dude, we're doing this next year!" He smiled at me, laughed doubtfully and seemed to take a moment to think through what I had just said. From what I recall, he nodded and said, "All right, let's do it."

THE EARLY YEARS

I had a goal and I was inspired: I wanted to cook just like the guys we had met that Sunday at the barbecue competition. At the time I didn't even know the word *pitmaster,* nor did I have even the slightest idea as to what it would take in effort, time or cash to pull it off. But I knew I had to do it.

Glenn practised with me, and we shared notes and strategies as we smoked up our neighbourhoods. Only a short nine months after that day trip, House of Q was born and we registered for our first competition. We didn't know what to bring, but we figured that bringing everything was the best idea. We both emptied our houses of tables, chairs, tents, knives, brushes, coolers and containers and packed them into several vans to set up at the competition site. Little did we know, we'd never need most of that stuff.

We prepared our dishes and cooked through the entire night as we'd planned, and in the morning the judges received our first competition tray. The category was pulled pork. I remember our entry being tough and undercooked, but I hoped it would be considered at least a valiant effort. An hour later we submitted our second tray, beef brisket. Our entry was tender and juicy; however, it was *over*cooked. And I had no idea how to present the meat: our slices were so big they didn't even fit into the Styrofoam tray, so I curled them up, crammed them into the tray and sent it off. Then I immediately started working on our third entry, chicken. I remember it looked good and tasted great—at least I thought it did. As to what the judges would say, we would have to wait and see. Our fourth and last entry was ribs, which we thought were good, but we didn't know if good was good enough. After we got our last tray to the judging area, we knew we'd done it. We'd successfully cooked at a barbecue

competition and got our trays to the judges on time. We'd reached a competition barbecue milestone: we had cooked our first event. Every competition cook remembers the first event.

Later that afternoon at the awards ceremony, we sat with friends who'd come to support us. The emcee called forward, one by one, the winning teams for pulled pork, starting with sixth place, then fifth and so on until he named the first-place team. Our name wasn't called. Then, the awards were presented for brisket. Our team wasn't called for that category either. But we didn't care. We just wanted to know, at the end of the event, that we had not finished in last place overall. That was our simple goal: we wanted to know we could cook and compete and beat at least one team. It was a humble goal. Maybe.

As the awards for chicken were announced, again starting with sixth place, then fifth and fourth, our team was called to the stage! I jolted my head upward, looking around as I processed the information and made sure I had heard what I thought I'd heard, and then I remember jumping from my chair, yelling, pumping my fist in the air and yelling some more. I danced all the way to the stage and even contemplated doing a cartwheel, which I really am glad I didn't follow through on. Woohoo! We had earned our first ribbon! A third place for chicken! With a massive smile on my face, I shook the emcee's hand, grabbed the white ribbon and held it in the air like it was the Super Bowl trophy. What a feeling!

I could hardly sit and listen to the rest of the awards ceremony. My heart was still pounding, and I couldn't care less about anything else. I leaned over to Glenn and said, "Dude, we got a ribbon!" Finally I managed to settle down a bit

Canadian Festival of Chili & Barbecue

Presente

webe

JUDGING AREA

as the awards for the final category, ribs, were being announced. House of Q was called to the stage again! We'd earned a sixth place for our rib entry. It was our second ribbon! At our first event! After the awards ceremony, we went to shake Ron Shewchuk's hand. By now he was a friend, and he, too, was competing at the event. We told him that for our award-winning entry, we had used the recipe for the ribs in his newly published cookbook, *Barbecue Secrets*. It's hard to know how good the recipes from a cookbook will be, but, in this instance, thank you, Ron! I smiled for weeks after our first-ever competition and told anyone who asked how things had gone. Ten years after that event, I am still sharing the story and I am still excited about it.

BUT THERE'S MORE

We continued to go to competitions; in fact, as many as we could. And our team continued to win awards at every competition. At the end of our second season, I got a phone call from Sandra Merk, the coordinator of the demonstration stage at the Vancouver Home + Design Show. She asked if Glenn and I would be interested in doing a demonstration of competition BBQ at the show. All I could think was, "You mean there is an audience that wants to hear what we do?" But I agreed anyway.

A month or so after the trade show, I got another phone call. This time it was Global TV news anchor Lynn Colliar asking if we would be interested in recording a few barbecue tips for the morning news broadcast. Eight of them, in fact. It wasn't even two years since our first competition, and already we had an opportunity to share our love of barbecue on TV. Even more people wanted to hear what we had to share. Since that summer, and for eight years now, I have been doing barbecue tips on Global TV, and I have had regular guest cooking segments in many different cities on many different TV stations. Newspapers and magazines have featured interviews about House of Q, and I have done cooking demonstrations at trade shows all over the country. Thousands of students have attended my cooking classes and learned from my experience as a competition-BBQ pitmaster and as a backyard cook. It's touching and humbling to know people want to learn what comes naturally to you.

EVER FEEL SCARED TO JUMP?

At competitions, after we have sent our trays to the barbecue judges, we have "leftovers." In fact, we knowingly cook far more than we need to because we are very selective about what we put in our trays for the judges. Our leftovers are then sampled by the public—and it was when people were sampling our barbecue that we first heard that they loved our sauce. They actually wouldn't leave our table. They asked how could they get some of the sauce to take home. I knew it tasted good, but I didn't understand that people would want to take it home to enjoy.

The first version of Apple Butter BBQ Sauce was a recipe that I knew I could re-create consistently over and over. But there were a lot of things I didn't know. How do you put it in a jar so you can sell it? How big a batch should I make? How do you get it into stores so that more people can taste and buy it? Was I up to creating a barbecue sauce company, I wondered. Was I an entrepreneur?

In early 2007, with a tremendous amount of stress (like many entrepreneurs who decide to move forward with their idea), we bottled our first barbecue sauce—Apple Butter BBQ Sauce. Our business goal was to simply raise some money to pay for our growing competition-BBQ hobby. Between the growing awareness of House of Q and the TV coverage, we got our sauces into stores and people bought them. Then those stores called us back and asked if we had more . . . The next year we added two more products—Slow Smoke Gold BBQ Sauce and Slather, and House Rub. We added one more sauce, Sugar & Spice BBQ Sauce, and finally, in the spring of 2010, I anxiously made the decision to quit my stable, long-term software job to focus on my growing business. I jumped. I made barbecue my primary occupation. Trust me, I hesitated. I analyzed the idea, slept on it, thought about it and went for walks to think even more about it. But, I'm glad I jumped. Some days I still can't believe I did it, but I did.

AND STILL THERE'S MORE

Barbecue has now become my career, both as a competitive cook and as an entrepreneur creating, selling and marketing barbecue sauces and spices. As you will see throughout this book, many of the recipes we share use our sauces and spices as an ingredient. While we win awards using these products, what's exciting is hearing from our fans about what they have learned and how their guests have reacted to the dishes they've cooked using our techniques and/or our products. Last week, for example, a lady walked up to me smiling and said, "You taught me how to cook ribs, and I won our neighbourhood rib cook-off!" A gentleman, Paul, proudly told me that he'd cooked my recipe for Handmade Italian Sausage Burgers (page 36) for a group at work and his colleagues had raved about them, making him look like a grill hero. People have also told me they've driven hours to a store to get a couple of jars of our sauces. "You drove three hours just to get some barbecue sauce?" I always want to put my hand over my heart and say, "Wow!"

After years of sharing BBQ tips and having our products in the market, I seem to have an endless number of stories, which is a good thing. After all, I did say that I like stories. Writing this cookbook has made me reflect on the journey I have been on and the most important lessons I've both learned and taught. Most of all, it's helped me identify what I hope this book will help you achieve. I'd love for you to be inspired just like I have been. I'd love for you to be brave, bold and strong enough to try just as I have. I'd love for you to share what you create with your family, friends, neighbours, guests and any other takers. Have an open and inviting heart. And lastly, I encourage you to celebrate. Celebrate the steps you take as you try to cook something new. Celebrate the things you learn. Celebrate the smiles and the admiration of your guests when they lick barbecue sauce from their fingers.

GRILL
LIKE
A PRO

SECRETS FOR BARBECUE SUCCESS

SCHOOL TEACHERS SOMETIMES SUMMARIZE A WHOLE YEAR OF MATERIAL IN ONE WORD: FUNDAMENTALS. THE YEAR'S CURRICULUM, LESSON AFTER LESSON, IS BUILT UPON THE FUNDAMENTAL SKILLS, OR BUILDING BLOCKS, THAT LEAD TO EDUCATIONAL SUCCESS. GRILLING MASTERY IS LIKE THAT TOO. . . THERE ARE FUNDAMENTAL TECHNIQUES THAT YOU MAY ALREADY BE DOING WHEN YOU COOK BUT THAT YOU MAY NOT EVEN BE AWARE OF. HERE I WANT TO SHARE SOME OF MY BEST TIPS AND TECHNIQUES SO THAT YOU CAN BECOME A BETTER COOK AT THE GRILL.

TOOLS OF THE TRADE

Over the years of cooking at competitive barbecue events and, of course, grilling steaks in the backyard, there are a few things I've learned about equipment. The most common cooking device in many backyards is a gas grill; here are my top three features to consider when looking for one:

1. THE CASE In the past 5 to 10 years, shiny, low-cost gas grills have become very popular. Although they often heat up nicely, once the lid is opened and the heat escapes, these inexpensive grills struggle to return to their original cooking temperature. For energy efficiency and best results, make sure the actual cooking chamber of the grill—the case—is made from a high-quality steel, stainless steel, ceramic or another solid material that will retain heat. Inexpensive grills have the cheapest price tag for a reason: they are made with cheap materials and they struggle to perform.

2. THE GRILL GRATES Depending on the manufacturer or even the retailer, you may be presented with options for different types of grill grates for your new grill. These include cast iron (which can also be coated with enamel or porcelain) and stainless steel. Cast-iron grates (uncoated) are perfect for searing; however, if you do not clean and oil them properly, your meats will stick. Enamel- or porcelain-coated cast-iron grates prevent meats from sticking and they are low maintenance, but all that expansion and contraction from the heat can, in time, break down the coating. Stainless steel grates are excellent for all-around use, and though they need a good coat of oil from time to time, they can generally be brushed clean and work very well. I like stainless steel grates for my gas grill.

3. THE BURNERS Many companies advertise how hot their grills are by referencing British Thermal Units, or BTUs. One BTU is the energy it takes to heat one pound of water by one degree Fahrenheit, but this measurement can be easily misinterpreted. As far as I'm concerned, a grill rated for 80,000 BTUs just means it will consume more fuel and energy than a comparable 45,000 BTU one; it does not mean it is a better grill. What's more important is the number of burners. More than two burners means more flexibility for hot and cool zones as you cook, so ignore the BTU rating.

Dedicated smokers (as opposed to using your gas grill as a smoker) are becoming increasingly popular, and there are several different technologies to contemplate. The most common options are gas (propane), charcoal, wood and pellet smokers. Each of these has benefits and drawbacks. I prefer a charcoal smoker for flavour; however, I also like the convenience of a pellet smoker. I encourage you to see what is available in your local stores and learn what might be best for your backyard.

In addition to having a great grill or smoker at your disposal, there are a few key tools every griller should have. These will increase your confidence when you cook and allow you to get great results.

A DIGITAL INSTANT-READ THERMOMETER: Whether you choose a single stick-probe, a fork, a wired cable thermometer or a wireless one that sends a message to your cell phone, make sure it tells you the actual temperature—a number, that is—and it is quick to respond. Never use the meat thermometers that oversimplify the task by listing different types of meat in the dial or by using words like *medium* and *well-done!* There nothing more frustrating than waiting for a thermometer that takes its sweet time to produce a temperature reading. I have a number of different thermometers, and I use them pretty much every time I am cooking—even when I am cooking bread.

A PAIR OF TONGS Forgo the lovely boxed sets of grill tools and accessories for a pair of simple, long-handled, stainless steel tongs. These are the best and most useful tool for turning and checking meats on the grill and the only one you *really* need. As for the rest of the tools in the gift box, I still don't know what to do with them.

A GRILL BRUSH Good cooks know that cleanliness is a key to success, and when grilling, that means making sure your grill is clean, especially the grates. Use a brass wire–bristled brush for cast-iron or coated grates and a stainless steel wire–bristled brush for stainless steel. In either case, choose a wooden handle; it is more heat-resistant than plastic, which can melt and cause the bristles to fall out of the brush.

ALUMINUM FOIL It seems you can never have enough heavy-duty foil around for wrapping or holding foods as you cook them, catching drips under the grill grate or even crumpling into a ball to clean off a grate in a pinch.

OIL FOR THE GRATES To help maintain your grill grates and prevent foods from sticking, you will need some oil. There is little need to use premium oils such as olive oil. When your grill gets hot, these oils simply burn and can add an off flavour to whatever you are cooking. Use oils that have a higher "smoke point," such as canola, sunflower, peanut or soybean oil. Apply the oil by wiping the grates with a paper towel soaked in oil, or buy an inexpensive spray bottle, fill it with oil and then spray the grates before you cook.

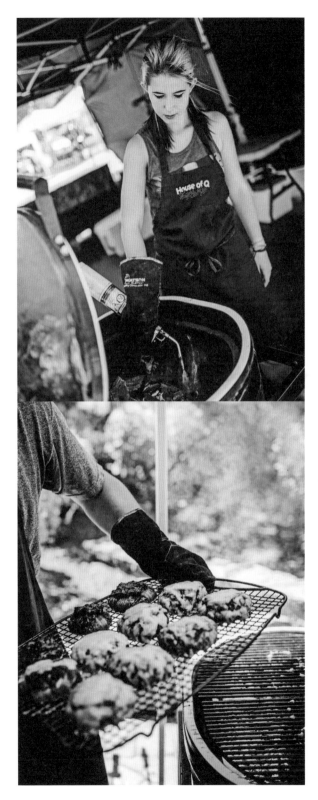

TIPS AND TECHNIQUES

One of the keys to learning the fundamentals is understanding barbecue terms and principles. As you read the recipes in this book, I'll describe various techniques that are needed to cook the dish properly. Here are some explanations to help you achieve optimal results.

GRILL IT! DIRECT VS. INDIRECT HEAT

Our natural reaction when cooking over a fire is to place the food right on top of the flame. This is called *direct cooking,* and it means the heat is directed straight toward the food. Direct cooking is great for foods such as steaks and burgers, where the desired result is meat that is caramelized and evenly seared on the surface and that has grill marks. It's not such a good choice for meats that may char on the outside in the intense heat before they are fully cooked on the inside.

In many instances, cooking food beside the heat source can provide better results. This is called *indirect cooking,* and it involves heating one side of the grill but not the other and, for the most part, cooking with the lid of the grill closed. Meats are placed on the cool side of the grill, and with the lid closed, the heat generated by the fire side is dispersed throughout the case. Note that on some grills there will be a deflector plate or another means of redirecting the heat so whatever you are cooking will not be directly above the heat source. Indirect cooking is particularly useful for foods that need more time to cook through or for items that cannot withstand the intensity of direct heat and therefore burn easily.

Master grillers know exactly when to use each of these techniques to get the right results, and each of the recipes in the book specifies whether to use direct or indirect cooking.

MODERATE THE HEAT!

Despite the fact that most grills now have a range of options for setting and adjusting the temperature of the grill, we've all seen cooks fire up the backyard grill, turn the heat dial to maximum and jump back as flames come shooting out the bottom, the sides and the top of the unit. And any food placed on the grill comes out charred, crusty and undercooked. The lesson here is that master grillers are always in control of the heat when they cook, and they adjust the temperature of the grill—often turning *down* the heat—to suit the food they're cooking. The big lesson here is that most foods, almost all in fact, are grilled at a low to medium temperature rather than at high heat.

Your grill may have a thermometer built into the lid that tells you the temperature of the cooking chamber. Often, however, these thermometers are not as accurate as you think, so here is a foolproof way to ensure the temperature of your grill. Start by warming up your grill to the desired temperature for a few minutes (or longer depending on the type of grill). Carefully lift the lid, hold your hand a couple of inches directly above the grate and start counting.

LOW HEAT If you can place your hand directly above the grate and hold it there for five seconds, that's low heat (250°F to 300°F).

MEDIUM HEAT If you can place your hand above the grate and hold it there for three seconds, that's medium heat (350°F to 375°F).

HIGH HEAT If you can't place your hand anywhere near the grate, then seemingly obviously, that is high heat (450°F+).

SMOKING HEAT When a recipe calls for smoking heat, it means cooking indirectly at low heat (usually in the range of 200°F to 300°F).

SMOKE IT!

Smoking foods is a fantastic way to add more flavour to grilled foods. It always involves cooking indirectly, away from the heat, and usually at a low temperature.

To set up your gas or propane grill to smoke meats, preheat one side of the grill to low or medium heat; leave the other side off. These days, gas grills often have a sliding tray or box in the cooking chamber that holds wood chips to smoke, so fill it with your choice of wood and add some flavour to whatever you are cooking. If you don't have this feature on your grill, tightly wrap the wood chips in aluminum foil, carefully lift the grate above the hot burner and place this packet under the grate but directly over the heat. The smoke will make its way out of the foil and into your grill. (You may find it helpful to leave the grate off the grill in this area to make placing the packet of chips easier; it will also force you to cook foods on the "cold," or indirect, side of the grill.) Close the lid and keep it shut to make your grill into an oven with the smoky air circulating on the inside.

If you have a charcoal cooker, place chips, chunks or even sticks of seasoned wood directly on top of your charcoal. I use only a handful or two of chips when smoking this way, but experiment to see what quantity produces the best results for you.

You can also try soaking the wood chips before placing them in your grill. Some people feel the soaked wood smoulders longer before it turns to ash. Others feel that soaking the wood chips simply delays the actual smoking process because wet wood doesn't burn. Personally, I don't soak my wood chips. Instead, I place them directly on the lit charcoal or in foil packets in my gas grill. The choice, however, is yours, and it gives you an opportunity to experiment.

A number of woods can be used for smoking. Traditional woods include oak, hickory or even mesquite. "Sweeter" options include maple, apple, alder or cherry. Each wood provides a different smoke flavour and colour, so experiment by starting with a small amount of a single wood and take notes as to what results you get. Over time, vary how many and what types of chips you use and how long you smoke each food. Everyone has different preferences, so figure out what works best for you.

COOK IT RIGHT!

A good, accurate digital thermometer is how backyard cooks become masters. Although the old adages like Grandma's "cook it until the juices run clear" or Mom's "cook it until the leg moves loosely" are good guidelines, science repeatedly proves these "rules" leave plenty of room for improvement. When the juice runs clear from chicken or burgers, the internal temperature of the meat can still be too low, meaning that it is not yet fully cooked. And when the leg of a chicken or turkey is loose, it means the bird is so overcooked that there is nothing left to hold it together. So, to properly know when foods are cooked, probe the meat with a digital thermometer, and then exude confidence to your friends when you declare, "Almost done!"

Having a good thermometer is the first step, but learning to use it properly is equally important. Remember that the temperature is measured at the tip of the probe, not at the tapered part of the thermometer or halfway up its shaft. Knowing that, make sure the tip is where you want to measure the doneness, such as right in the middle of the chicken breast rather than on the bone, or in the middle of the burger rather than near the grill grate. I often check multiple points of whatever

I am cooking. As an example, when I am cooking a whole chicken, I will check both the thighs and the breasts for doneness, and if I am cooking several pieces of meat, such as a whole bunch of pork chops, I will check each one individually rather than checking one and declaring all of them done. But remember, wherever the tip of the thermometer is, that is where it is reading the temperature.

GLAZE IT!

A key ingredient in barbecue sauces is sugar, whether it be common white and brown sugars, honey, molasses or even fruit. These sugars provide flavour but also help the sauce to stick to meats and give them a beautiful caramelized finish. Knowing when to glaze is a skill a good griller needs to learn. Use sweeter sauces that have a higher sugar content toward the end of the cooking time—a rule of thumb is about three-quarters of the way through—so they melt and caramelize on whatever you are cooking but don't burn. House of Q Apple Butter BBQ Sauce and our Sugar & Spice BBQ Sauce are examples of "sugary" sauces. Other sauces, such as those with a vinegar base, like House of Q Rock'n Red BBQ Sauce or Slow Smoke Gold BBQ Sauce and Slather, can be used as a glaze or earlier in the cooking process as a marinade.

GIVE IT A REST!

A quick science lesson explains what happens to food as it cooks and why allowing meats to rest is a good thing. When we expose foods to heat over a flame on a grill, in boiling liquids or even directly on a hot pan, we are increasing the pressure surrounding the food. This increase in pressure makes proteins in particular tighten as they cook. Think of proteins as coiled springs that tighten as the pressure on them increases. When a meat is

"well done," those springs are tightened as much as they will go.

Removing meat from the heat actually reduces the pressure on the proteins, which allows them to relax. Think of it as going on vacation after getting all stressed out at work . . . just like your body releases its tension, the meat lets go of all its cooking stress. When proteins are allowed to rest, they loosen up and become more tender. The loosening fibres allow moisture within the meat (which is actually dissolved collagen) to move around freely; if there is too much moisture that's not distributed throughout the meat, it will flow out (called purge). So, allowing meats to rest gives them time to become more tender and juicy, which makes for a better eating experience.

How long meats should rest depends on their size. An eight-ounce steak or a chicken breast will only need a few minutes to relax, whereas a 15-pound turkey can rest for an hour or more. As a guideline, think about how long it has been cooking and with how much energy. A whole turkey takes a long time and plenty of energy to cook, thus it can handle a longer resting period than a chicken breast that cooked in 30 minutes.

ESSENTIALS OF FLAVOUR

Tools and techniques are important, but an essential, and often overlooked, fundamental is understanding and appreciating flavour. You've been shopping for fresh ingredients, you've planned a great meal, but your skills as a cook will really shine when you understand flavour.

Be inspired by all of your senses—every one of them. Master cooks *look* for ingredients with an appealing colour, a perfectly caramelized surface and a finished dish that's so visually tempting that guests want to dig in. Grill masters *listen* for the sound of a chicken's skin crisping or a steak searing on the grill, and from the sizzling and popping they know exactly when the meat is at the right temperature and properly caramelized. Grill masters *feel* for tenderness and for doneness with a gentle touch of their tongs—or they may use their fingers to feel for creaminess or, at times, a slight, desirable toughness. They *smell* for an enticing aroma that draws eaters in. And, of course, they constantly *taste* for the perfect level of acidity, salt-iness or seasoning; the perfect texture; the combined sensation in the mouth of everything that is in the dish; and even umami, what the Japanese describe as the fifth taste. Our senses are our best tools to create great dishes, and I encourage you to develop or strengthen your ability to use each one of them as you cook.

Many of the recipe methods in this book deliberately do not provide precise cooking times. I don't cook this way, and I want to encourage you to look for colour, feel for texture and listen for doneness rather than counting out a certain number of minutes. Trust me, you'll become a better cook this way.

One more thing about flavour. Many of the recipes in this book call for House of Q barbecue sauces or spices. They will add fantastic flavour to these dishes—and mostly anything you cook on the grill. However, I don't want you to get halfway through a dish and stop because you don't have one of our products. They are available in many stores across the country and online (houseofq. com); but, you can still make these dishes without them. A sauce is just a sauce, right? If a recipe calls for our award-winning Apple Butter BBQ Sauce, a smoky applesauce-based sauce with plenty of molasses and a tiny hint of pepper, try your favourite fruit-based barbecue sauce as a substitute. The Slow Smoke Gold BBQ Sauce and Slather is our award-winning version of a Carolina-style mustard sauce, and it is tangy, bright and mustard-based with a peppery finish. There are many mustard-based barbecue sauces, but you can even use prepared yellow mustard in its place. Our Sugar & Spice BBQ Sauce is our spiciest sauce, and it starts with the sweet flavours of molasses and honey and then becomes spicy with cayenne pepper to finish. So, a spicy barbecue sauce might be a good replacement. The Rock'n Red BBQ Sauce is a mild but tangy vinegar-and-tomato-based sauce with a slight pepper finish. It's our closest thing to a classic barbecue sauce, so seek out your favourite barbecue sauce, and use it instead. And the House Rub is a sweet, salty and fragrant mix of spices that can be tailored by adding one or two of your own favourite spices. Use another rub if you don't have ours.

Now that you have the basics about equipment, the keys to proper grilling techniques and a willingness to play with flavours, you're all set to start cooking. So fire up your grill, pick out a handful of recipes and let's get started!

APPETIZERS

WHETHER YOU WANT TO FEED A CROWD, A FAMILY OR A FEW FRIENDS WHILE YOU WAIT FOR ANOTHER ROUND OF FOOD, APPETIZERS CAN FIT THE BILL. YOU CAN EVEN MAKE A WHOLE MEAL OF APPETIZERS. SOME OF THESE FAVOURITE RECIPES ARE REALLY EASY, AND THEY WILL IMPRESS YOUR GUESTS; OTHERS WILL ALLOW YOU TO "UP YOUR GRILL GAME."

CEDAR-PLANKED BRIE
WITH CRANBERRY CHUTNEY

Who can resist warm, smoky, melted cheese? When it's served over crackers or fresh bread, you might even be tempted to skip the main course... For tips on cooking with planks, see Planks and Grill Stones (page 96). If you're in a hurry, you can make the cranberry chutney ahead of time on the stove.

2½ cups fresh or frozen cranberries

½ to ⅓ cup House of Q Sugar & Spice BBQ Sauce or your favourite thick, sweet and spicy barbecue sauce

½ cup maple syrup

1 cedar plank, unsoaked

1 wheel of Brie or Camembert cheese, 4 to 6 inches in diameter

Crackers or slices of fresh bread

Place the cranberries, BBQ sauce and maple syrup in a sauté pan over medium heat on your stovetop, grill side-burner or even on the grill, and cook, stirring often. Once the cranberries begin to soften, press them with the back of a spoon. Once most of the berries have burst, 10 to 20 minutes, remove the pan from the heat and allow the mixture to cool. Spoon the thickened chutney into an airtight container and refrigerate until ready to use.

Prepare your grill for direct grilling, medium-high heat. When the grill is hot, rinse the plank under cold running water and place it on the grate. Close the lid and allow the plank to heat for 4 or 5 minutes or until it starts to crackle. Reduce the heat to medium-low and place the cheese on the plank, and then close the lid and cook for 8 to 10 minutes, possibly longer. Open the lid and scoop a generous portion of cranberry chutney onto the warming cheese, close the lid and cook until the cheese is puffing out but not burst. Transfer the cheese on the plank to a metal or glass plate, and serve immediately with crackers (or fresh bread).

CHICKEN AND PRAWN
LETTUCE WRAPS

Lettuce wraps are nice and versatile because your guests can pick and choose what they want to put in them and how much. They also look beautiful served family-style on a plate. This recipe requires a bit of advance preparation and skill with timing. Begin marinating the chicken a day ahead of time, and have the chicken and the vegetables ready to go before you light the grill. If the prawns are small, have some skewers or a grill basket on hand to cook them. You want to put the ingredients on the grill in the right order so that it all comes together, ready to eat, at the same time. Serve these wraps with your favourite white wine.

---

1 to 2 lbs boneless chicken thighs, skin on or skinless

½ to 1 cup Italian or vinaigrette-style salad dressing or House of Q Slow Smoke Gold BBQ Sauce

1 to 2 red bell peppers, quartered

1 to 2 fennel bulbs, rinsed and quartered

1 to 2 Tbsp olive oil

Salt and black pepper

½ cup House of Q Apple Butter BBQ Sauce or your favourite sauce for chicken

1 lb prawns, peeled (and deveined, if large)

1 bunch green onions, diced

1 head butter or iceberg lettuce, separated into leaves

1 lemon or lime, cut into wedges

Place the chicken in a large resealable bag, and add the salad dressing (or Slow Smoke Gold BBQ Sauce). Seal the bag tightly, squeeze the marinade until the chicken is well coated and allow the mixture to marinate, refrigerated, overnight.

When you are ready to cook, prepare your grill for direct grilling, medium heat. Brush or wipe the grates with oil, if necessary. Place the peppers and fennel in a bowl. Drizzle with half the olive oil and sprinkle with salt and pepper. Place the prawns in a separate bowl, drizzle them with the remaining olive oil and sprinkle with salt and pepper. If the prawns are small, thread them onto skewers or place them in a grill basket.

Depending on the size of your grill, cook each ingredient at the same time or in batches. Start with the chicken. Remove the chicken from the marinade, shaking off any excess, and place the pieces directly on the grill. Once the chicken has some colour on one side, turn it over and continue cooking.

While the chicken is cooking, place the peppers and fennel on the grill. Sear until the vegetables show grill marks, and then turn them over. Cook them until they begin to soften but still have a slight crunch. The fennel may take longer than the peppers, depending on the size of the pieces.

Brush the chicken with the Apple Butter BBQ sauce (or your favourite sauce for chicken), and cook until the internal temperature of the meat reaches 165°F.

Just before serving, place the prawns on the grill. They will cook quickly. When they turn from grey to pink, remove them from the heat immediately or they will become rubbery.

Arrange the chicken, grilled vegetables, green onions, prawns and lettuce leaves on a large family-style platter. Pass around individual plates and wedges of lemon or lime, and allow guests to help themselves. Enjoy!

GRILLED BLACK BEAN AND MUSHROOM
BURRITOS

Wondering what you can make on the grill for guests who don't eat meat? Here is a vegetarian dish that is flavourful and a hit at many parties. If you're pressed for time, make the filling ahead of time on your stove, heat the tortillas on the grill, assemble and serve with a variety of sauces and dips, including Grilled Tomato Salsa (page 168), guacamole and sour cream. This recipe is also fantastic made into quesadillas instead of burritos, if you prefer.

1 to 2 Tbsp olive oil

1 small onion, diced

1 lb mushrooms, chopped

1 large can black beans, drained and rinsed

2 to 3 Tbsp House of Q House Rub
    or your favourite barbecue seasoning

3 to 4 Tbsp roughly chopped
    fresh oregano or cilantro

1 to 2 cups grated Monterey Jack cheese

4 to 6 large or 12 small flour tortillas

Heat the olive oil in a sauté pan over medium on your grill side-burner or on your stove. Add the onions and sauté until soft, about 5 minutes. Stir in the mushrooms, cooking them until they begin to soften and release their moisture. Add the black beans and the rub, and stir until well combined. Remove from the heat and allow to cool to room temperature.

Stir in the oregano (or cilantro) and cheese. The filling can be covered and refrigerated until you are ready to use it.

Prepare your grill for direct grilling, medium heat. Place the tortillas directly on the grill, and warm them for a few seconds. Remove them from the heat, and then spoon ½ to 1 cup of the filling in the centre of the tortilla. Fold the left and right sides of the tortilla over the filling, and then fold the bottom edge up over the filling and tightly roll the rest of the tortilla to form a wrapped burrito.

Place the burritos, seam side down, on the grate and cook until grill marks appear. Turn the burritos over and cook for another couple of minutes, or until the filling is completely heated through. If you want to get grill marks all around the burritos, roll them every few minutes. Serve whole or cut in half, with your favourite toppings.

BALLS OF WONDERMENT

This dish could have been called bacon-wrapped meatballs, but I like the long, dramatic-sounding title better. There are many variations of this idea on the competition-BBQ circuit, where they are often known as *moink balls* ("moo" + "oink"). Whatever you name them, these savoury bites are quick to make, sinfully addictive and perfect served with plenty of beer or a summer cocktail. Make sure the bacon is thinly sliced, or the bacon will still be underdone by the time the meatballs are cooked.

---

2 lbs ground beef

2 Tbsp House of Q House Rub or
your favourite beef seasoning

2 cloves garlic, minced

2 tsp minced fresh rosemary

1 lb bacon, cut in thin slices

½ to 1 cup House of Q Sugar & Spice
BBQ Sauce or your favourite
barbecue sauce

In a large bowl, mix the ground beef with the rub (or beef seasoning), garlic and rosemary until well combined. Form the mixture into 1- to 1½-inch meatballs and set them on a plate. (You should have about 25 to 30 meatballs.) Wrap a slice of bacon around each meatball, holding it in place with a toothpick, if needed. (If the bacon slices are long, cut them in half before wrapping the meatballs.)

Prepare your grill for indirect cooking on medium heat. Place a foil tray or a sheet of aluminum foil under the grate on the cool side of the grill to catch the bacon drippings. Place the wrapped meatballs on the cool side of the grill, close the lid and cook for 30 to 45 minutes, or until the internal temperature of the meatballs has reached 140°F.

Pour the BBQ sauce into a large bowl. Working in batches, add a few of the meatballs to the bowl and gently stir to coat them. Return the meatballs to the grill. Alternatively, if you think the bacon wrap will come apart, brush the meatballs with the glaze while they are on the grill. The meatballs are done when the glaze has set, the bacon is thoroughly cooked and the meat has reached an internal temperature of 160°F.

Transfer the cooked meatballs to a platter or bowl, and serve them with toothpicks or skewers.

A barbecue rub provides a fundamental layer of flavour in any dish, and it can be the difference between a good dish and an award-winning one. When I first entered barbecue competitions, I used to make a new rub for each individual dish I prepared. I made pork rubs, brisket rubs, chicken rubs and rib rubs. However, I soon learned that rubs are mostly created from the same ingredients: salt, sugar, paprika and maybe onion, garlic and pepper. From there, each rub has a few of its own characteristic seasonings to make it special.

House of Q House Rub is our version of a rub base, a combination of spices that can be used right out of the jar or added to with other seasonings. Say you want a fragrant pork dish—pour some House Rub into a bowl, add some cinnamon and cumin and mix well to make your fragrant rub. Or maybe you are cooking a prime rib roast. (See Father's Day Prime Rib [page 68] for a perfect example of "doctoring" the House Rub.) Pour some House Rub into a bowl, add a bit of garlic and rosemary to it and you've got a beef rub. We've had fans of our rub say they put it on everything from scrambled eggs to popcorn to french fries and even in a Caesar cocktail. Think of a rub as a great way to season and add flavour to just about any food.

HOUSE OF Q
HOUSE RUB
STORY

DINOSAUR EGGS

These large stuffed mini-meatloafs are sure to impress your guests or your family, and they are easy to make. To help moderate the heat from the jalapeño peppers, scrape out and discard the seeds and the soft white membrane inside.

1 small onion, finely diced

2 cloves garlic, minced

3 Tbsp dried oregano

3 Tbsp dried basil

2 to 3 Tbsp seasoned salt

1 Tbsp black pepper

2 to 3 lbs ground turkey or chicken
(2 lbs makes 5 "eggs")

1 block (8 oz) cream cheese, room temperature

1 cup grated cheddar cheese

1 lb bacon, fried until crisp, cooled and chopped

5 to 8 jalapeño peppers, halved lengthwise, seeded and membranes removed

½ to 1 cup House of Q Apple Butter BBQ Sauce or your favourite smoky barbecue sauce

Place the onions, garlic, oregano, basil, salt, pepper and ground turkey (or chicken) in a large clean bowl. Mix thoroughly until well combined, and then refrigerate for 1 hour to allow the flavours to infuse the meat.

In a separate bowl, mix the cream cheese, cheddar cheese and bacon together using a spoon. The mixture will be thick and hard to stir, but be patient. Using a teaspoon, spoon the cheese mixture into the jalapeño halves, and then press the halves together to re-form a whole pepper.

Remove the turkey (or chicken) mixture from the fridge, and divide it into 5 to 8 portions (depending on the number of peppers you have). Using your hands, press the meat into a thin patty, about ¼ inch thick. Place a cheese-filled pepper in the middle of the patty, and then roll the meat around the jalapeño, completely encasing it to form an "egg." Repeat with the remaining jalapeños and turkey (or chicken).

Prepare your grill for indirect cooking, medium heat. Place the dinosaur eggs on the cool side of the grill, close the lid and cook for 30 to 50 minutes, or until the internal temperature of the meat reaches 165°F. For extra flavour, brush the cooked eggs with the BBQ sauce when the meat reaches 145°F. Serve these whole and surprise your guests, or slice them to show off the pepper and the cheese on the inside.

BACON
BITES

House of Q partnered with CFOX, a local Vancouver radio station, to offer a free barbecue breakfast in different locations each Friday morning. Billed as the "world's largest FREE drive-through BBQ," the promotion drew thousands of listeners who lined up for miles to sample the food, help raise funds for the Make-A-Wish foundation and participate in the antics that ensued during the live broadcast of *The Jeff O'Neil Show*. We crafted this dish for one of these events, and it truly represents indulgence—or as Jeff O'Neil put it: "I'm not sure if *pork-gasm* is a word yet, but maybe it should be."

---

1 slab of cured bacon, 2 to 3 lbs (or more)

3 to 4 Tbsp House of Q House Rub or your favourite pork rub

4 to 6 Tbsp House of Q Rock'n Red BBQ Sauce or your favourite tangy barbecue sauce

Prepare your grill for indirect smoking, low heat. Place a sheet of aluminum foil under the cool side to catch the bacon drippings. Place a foil packet of wood chips under the grill grate on the hot side of the grill.

Cut the bacon into long ¾-inch-thick slices. Place the bacon strips on the cool side of the grill, and smoke them for 45 to 60 minutes, or until the fat has started to render. Sprinkle both sides of the bacon with the rub, and continue to cook it for another 20 to 30 minutes. The bacon should be well rendered but not yet getting crisp.

To finish these tasty bites and add more flavour, brush each side of the bacon with the BBQ sauce, and move the strips to the hot side of the grill to caramelize the sauce. Once the glaze has set, remove the bacon from the grill, cut the strips into 1-inch cubes and arrange them on a platter. Serve them with skewers to make fancy hors d'oeuvres, or simply hand around some forks. Prepare for plenty of bacon comments.

I'M A COOK,
NOT YOUR DOCTOR

Trying to be healthy can be hard to do in the kitchen. This becomes clear when you experience the tasty goodness of things that are, in the end, not necessarily good for you. Many of my recipes use real butter, not margarine. They use bacon, liberally. They call for "regular" ground meat and not lean *because* it has more fat in it. The underlying principle is that fat equals flavour, and I cook to achieve award-winning flavour. If you take away the fat in the recipe, the flavour seems to disappear.

THERE ARE TWO LESSONS TO TAKE INTO ACCOUNT.

1. DO NOT EAT A FAT-INTENSE MEAL EVERY MEAL, EVERY DAY. Bacon-wrapped, cheese-stuffed burgers topped with sugary sauce are a meal that we indulge in only periodically. So, here's what I am saying . . . it's okay to eat a fatty meal and to enjoy it, as you should. The thing is to do it only once in a while. How often is for you to decide, but the answer is not every meal, every day.

2. SERVE PROTEINS, LIKE STEAKS, SLICED AND ON A PLATTER, FAMILY-STYLE. Some guests dropped into our house around dinner one day. It wasn't a planned visit, and I did have a couple of steaks in the fridge, but not enough for everyone. I didn't know whether to run to the store to get more, to make more side dishes or simply to fess up to my guests and say that the meal was going to be light on content. In the end I cooked the steaks as I planned, and, when they were resting on the cutting board, I decided to cut them into slices instead of serving them whole. I put all the pieces on a platter and served them to our guests along with some salads and side dishes. At the end of the meal, much to my surprise, there was leftover steak. It was a good lesson: if you want to eat a bit less, serve proteins, like steaks, sliced and set on a platter, family-style. Chances are people will eat less than if they were served a whole piece.

NO-FAIL
SMOKED CHICKEN WINGS

Chicken wings make a great appetizer, but it can be challenging for new grill cooks to ensure wings are properly cooked but not burned. Be creative with your ingredients and create your own flavour, but follow the technique in this recipe for guaranteed success! If you want to add more flavour, use maple or alder wood chips in your smoker, as these are perfect smoking woods for chicken.

Once you've mastered the cooking technique, try different glazes or marinades. Instead of the Apple Butter BBQ Sauce, mix equal parts of honey or maple syrup and House of Q Slow Smoke Gold BBQ Sauce for a sweet mustard flavour. Or look around your kitchen and come up with your own variation. Serve these wings with fresh-cut vegetables and cold beer.

2 to 3 lbs chicken wings, whole or in pieces
½ to 1 cup hot sauce (Tabasco or Frank's RedHot Sauce)
Salt and black pepper or House of Q House Rub
1 cup House of Q Apple Butter BBQ Sauce
    or your favourite smoky barbecue sauce

Place the chicken wings in a resealable plastic bag. Add the hot sauce ensuring that the chicken is evenly coated, seal the bag and allow the mixture to marinate, refrigerated, for a few hours or overnight.

Remove the wings from the bag, and spread them out on a baking sheet. Generously sprinkle the chicken with salt and pepper (or House Rub).

Prepare your grill for indirect cooking on medium heat. Place a foil packet of wood chips under the grill grate on the hot side of the grill. Arrange the wings on the cool side of the grill, close the lid and allow the chicken to smoke for 30 to 45 minutes. (If you have a large grill, you may need to replace the wood chips with another packet.) Once the wings have a dry "crust" and are about three-quarters cooked (the internal temperature of the meat reaches 145°F), they are ready to be glazed.

Pour the BBQ sauce into a large bowl, add the chicken wings and stir gently to coat them thoroughly. Return the wings to the cool side of the grill, close the lid and cook until the glaze is set and the wings reach an internal temperature of at least 165°F. The key to cooking chicken properly is to cook with indirect heat and at lower temperatures.

Serve these wings on a platter, family-style.

SAUSAGES AND BURGERS

MANY BRAND NEW GRILLS
ARE BROKEN IN BY COOKING
BURGERS, ONE OF NORTH
AMERICA'S MOST POPULAR
FOOD ITEMS. RESIST SHOPPING
IN THE FROZEN FOOD AISLE
AND BUYING THE PREFORMED
BURGERS THAT I CALL HOCKEY
PUCKS. INSTEAD, MAKE YOUR
OWN HOMEMADE SAUSAGES
AND BURGERS. YOU WILL BE
REWARDED!

HAND-MINCED CHICKEN AND SAGE
SAUSAGES

If you have made your own meatloaf or burgers, you can make your own sausages too. Here's a great recipe to get you started—and it makes a fantastic burger too! For this recipe, I prefer to mince chicken thighs with a knife because I often find that storebought ground chicken is too moist, and it's difficult to form sausages with it. But if you are in a pinch, use the store-bought stuff. Serve the cooked sausages with a great-tasting mustard like House of Q Slow Smoke Gold BBQ Sauce. Fried onions are an optional accompaniment, but beer is not!

1 Tbsp sea salt or kosher salt

2 tsp black pepper

1 Tbsp granulated garlic

1 Tbsp minced fresh sage

3 lbs skinless, boneless chicken thighs, hand-minced, or ground chicken

3 Tbsp white wine or ice water (optional)

In a large bowl, stir together the salt, pepper, granulated garlic and sage until well combined. Using your hands, mix the minced chicken into the spices. As the fibres in the meat begin to break apart, the mixture may become harder and harder to blend. If it becomes too tough and dry, add some wine (or ice water) a little bit at a time. Mix until the spices are evenly distributed throughout and the mixture has an even consistency.

Cut 3 pieces of plastic wrap, each about 14 to 16 inches long. Place one of them on a large cutting board. Take about one-third of the meat mixture, and set it on the plastic wrap. Using your hands, form the meat into a long log shape roughly 1½ to 2 inches in diameter. Fold the plastic wrap over the sausage, and then roll it away from you to enclose the meat. Gently roll the sausage on the board to even out the thickness all along its length. Repeat with the remaining sausage meat, and then refrigerate all 3 for at least 30 minutes while you clean up and prepare the rest of your meal.

Prepare your grill for direct grilling, medium heat. Brush or wipe the grates with oil, if necessary. Find the edge of the plastic wrap and unroll the sausages onto your grill. Discard the plastic wrap. Turn the sausages every few minutes until a cooked crust has formed on all sides. Don't scrape and prod the meat to release it from the grill or the sausages will fall apart—when a crust forms, the sausage will release from the grate. When the internal temperature of the meat reaches 165°F, 20 to 40 minutes total, transfer the sausages to a cutting board, and allow to rest for a few minutes (covered, if you choose).

To serve, slice on an angle to present great-tasting, handmade sausages.

BBQ BRIAN'S TOP FIVE TIPS FOR BETTER BURGERS

1. **USE DIFFERENT MEATS.** Try pork, turkey, chicken, lamb, venison or bison instead of the usual ground beef. Or try a different cut of beef—chuck, brisket or even sirloin can all be ground. Or mix different meats such as lamb and pork or pork and beef. Just imagine the combinations you can create!

2. **KEEP THE MEAT COLD.** Form the burger patties, and then allow them to rest for 30 minutes to an hour in the fridge or the freezer. This step gives the flavours time to come together and helps the burgers to retain their shape when cooked.

3. **BE CREATIVE WITH THE "CARRIERS."** Think beyond the usual bun, and slide your burgers onto pitas, tortillas, English muffins, waffles, sections of baguette or—for a lighter, gluten-free option—lettuce leaves.

4. **SKIP THE BINDER.** Mom's recipe may use an egg or bread crumbs as a binder, but instead massage a portion of the raw ground meat into a thick paste by breaking down the protein fibres. Mix that paste back into the rest of the meat mixture, and you've got a natural meat binder.

5. **STOP GUESSING.** Use a thermometer and make sure to cook all ground meats to between 160°F and 165°F. Don't overcook them or they will become dry and flavourless.

AND THREE BONUS TIPS

BE CREATIVE WITH THE SHAPES. Who said patties have to be round? Make them oblong or oval, sausage or meatball-shaped, just for fun.

ADD SAUCE. Great sauce adds flavour and moisture. Brush it on patties when they are about three-quarters cooked (about 140°F to 145°F) so it can caramelize on the outside, or mix it into the patties when you form them to add extra flavour.

THINK ARCHITECTURE. Big patty + small bun = disaster. Be sure the patty is the same size as the burger bun or just a little larger so that as it shrinks on the grill it will be the same size as the bun. Also, sautéed onions + lettuce = big mess. Plan your toppings and how they will "stick" together on the burger instead of sliding off the top or squeezing out the sides.

CHEESE-STUFFED BACON-WRAPPED
HOT DOGS

SERVES 6 TO 8

What says summer more than hot dogs? From the ball game to the backyard, no celebration is complete without these smoky treats that appeal to kids and adults alike. Here's my homemade version, dressed up a bit with cheese on the inside; it's a tribute to Chef Ted Reader, cookbook author, grilling guru and inspiration. Load up the cooked dogs with mustard, mayonnaise or barbecue sauce, and serve them topped with some Shaved Fennel and Onion Salad (page 139) and a handful of napkins!

2 lbs ground pork, chicken or turkey

2 Tbsp House of Q House Rub or your favourite barbecue seasoning

6 to 8 storebought cheese sticks (or cut your own from a block of mozzarella, Jarlsberg, Monterey Jack or cheddar cheese), each ½-inch × ½-inch × 4 to 6 inches

1 lb bacon, cut in thin slices (optional)

¼ cup House of Q Rock'n Red BBQ Sauce or your favourite tangy barbecue sauce

2 baguettes, sliced lengthwise

In a large bowl, mix together the ground meat and rub (or seasoning) until well combined. Divide the meat into 6 or 8 equal balls.

Place 1 ball on a cutting board and cover it with a layer of plastic wrap. Using a rolling pin, press the meat into a thin rectangle—the thinner the better. Remove the plastic wrap and set a cheese stick in the centre of the meat, and then roll up the ground meat around it, folding in the edges to seal in the cheese. If you choose, wrap a slice of bacon around each hot dog, arranging it in a spiral pattern from one end to the other. (Depending on the size of your hot dogs, you may need more than 1 slice of bacon to wrap each one.) Roll, fill and wrap the remaining dogs, and then arrange them on a plate, cover and refrigerate for 1 hour.

Prepare your grill for indirect cooking on medium heat. Place a sheet of aluminum foil under the cool side to catch the bacon drippings. Arrange the hot dogs on the cool side of the grill, close the lid and cook for 20 to 60 minutes, glazing them with the BBQ sauce when the internal temperature of the meat reaches 145°F. When it has reached 165°F, transfer them to a plate.

Cut the baguettes to the same length as the dogs. Smear your favourite condiments on the bread, add a cooked cheese dog and dig in!

HANDMADE ITALIAN
SAUSAGE BURGERS

One of my favourite sausages is the Italian variety, and this recipe also makes an amazing burger! It tastes great topped with cheese, grilled bell peppers, onions, pineapple or whatever ingredients you have on hand. Or use this recipe to make sausages just like the Hand-minced Chicken and Sage Sausages (page 32).

2 Tbsp sea salt or kosher salt

1 Tbsp black pepper

2 Tbsp granulated garlic

1 to 1½ Tbsp whole or ground
    fennel seeds (I prefer whole)

1 Tbsp crushed red pepper
    flakes (or more)

1 Tbsp paprika

1 tsp dried oregano

5 lbs ground pork

Red wine or ice water (optional)

10 to 15 soft fluffy buns,
    such as Portuguese or
    Italian rolls, cut in half

Line a baking sheet with waxed paper or parchment paper.

In a large bowl, stir together the salt, pepper, granulated garlic, fennel seeds, red pepper flakes, paprika and oregano until well combined. Using your hands, mix the ground pork into the spices. As the fibres in the meat begin to break apart, the mixture may become harder and harder to blend. If it becomes too tough and dry, add some wine (or ice water), a little bit at a time. Mix until the spices are evenly distributed throughout the meat. Divide the meat mixture into 10 to 15 equal portions, and form each one into a patty roughly ½ to ¾ inch thick. Place the formed patties on the baking sheet and freeze them for 30 minutes so the flavours can come together while you clean up and prepare your grill.

Prepare your grill for direct grilling, medium heat. Brush or wipe the grates with oil, if necessary. Place the burgers on the grill and sear them on each side, establishing their colour, until the internal temperature of the meat reaches 160°F to 165°F. Allow the burgers to rest for a couple of minutes. Slide the burgers onto individual buns, and serve with your favourite toppings.

BBQ BRIAN'S
BEEFY SLIDERS

I originally created this recipe as a "two-bite" burger, but you can easily turn these sliders into full-sized burgers. Serve these classic beef patties with your favourite toppings, such as onions, grilled bell peppers, tomatoes, lettuce and even sautéed mushrooms.

3 lbs ground beef

¼ cup soy sauce

2 Tbsp minced garlic

¼ cup finely chopped onions

2 Tbsp sesame oil

1 tsp sea salt or kosher salt

½ cup House of Q Slow Smoke Gold BBQ Sauce or your favourite prepared mustard

24 mini burger buns or 6 to 10 burger buns (I use ciabatta), sliced open

In a large bowl, combine the ground beef, soy sauce, garlic, onions, sesame oil and salt. Using your hands, mix until the seasonings are evenly distributed throughout the meat.

Line a baking sheet with waxed paper or parchment paper. If you are making small sliders, measure out 2 oz portions, or about 24 patties. For full-sized burgers, divide the meat into 6 to 10 equal balls, and then form each one into a patty of 4 to 6 oz each. Set the patties on the baking sheet, and place them in the freezer for 30 to 45 minutes so the flavours can come together while you clean up and prepare your grill.

Prepare your grill for direct grilling, medium heat. Brush or wipe the grates with oil, if necessary. Using a brush, smear both sides of each patty with the Slow Smoke Gold BBQ Sauce (or mustard). Place the sliders on the grill, and sear them on each side to establish their colour. The burgers are done when the internal temperature of the meat reaches 160°F. Allow the sliders to rest for a couple of minutes, and then slide them onto individual buns and serve with your favourite toppings.

JALAPEÑO 'N' CHEESE
CORNBREAD WAFFLE BURGERS

Ron Shewchuk is a Vancouver-based cookbook author, presenter and barbecue evangelist. Over the years, he has been an inspiration, a mentor, a friend and a fellow competitor. At a trade show in 2012, the two of us were invited to participate in a live battle of the burgers. As we stood on stage providing our best burger tips, we cooked two different burgers for a panel of judges. After eating my burger that day, Bryan Baeumler from HGTV, who was one of the celebrity judges, tweeted, "Just ate the best burger of my life!" Here's that life-changing recipe. It may seem like the whole kitchen and every ingredient in it is in this recipe . . . It's close but the end result is the prize.

BREAKFAST SAUSAGE BURGERS
1 Tbsp sea salt or kosher salt
1 Tbsp ground dried sage
1 tsp crushed red pepper flakes
½ tsp ground coriander
¼ tsp ground ginger
¼ tsp ground dried thyme
¼ tsp cayenne pepper
2 lbs ground pork
1 lb bacon, cut in thick slices
6 to 8 very thick slices
  aged cheddar cheese
6 to 8 eggs
¼ cup mayonnaise
2 to 4 Tbsp House of Q Slow Smoke
  Gold BBQ Sauce or your favourite
  prepared mustard

**JALAPEÑO 'N' CHEESE
CORNBREAD WAFFLES**
1 cup cornmeal
1 cup all-purpose flour
1 Tbsp baking powder
2 tsp sea salt or kosher salt
1 jalapeño pepper, seeded
  and finely chopped
½ to 1 cup grated aged cheddar cheese
4 large eggs
½ cup vegetable oil
1½ cups buttermilk

BREAKFAST SAUSAGE BURGERS Line a baking sheet with waxed paper or parchment paper.

In a large bowl, stir together the salt, sage, red pepper flakes, coriander, ginger, thyme and cayenne pepper until well combined. Using your hands, mix the ground pork into the spices until the spices are evenly distributed throughout the meat. Divide the meat mixture into 6 to 8 equal balls, and then form each one into a burger patty.

Arrange the patties on the baking sheet, and freeze them for 30 minutes so the flavours can meld while you clean up and then prepare the waffles, the bacon and your grill.

JALAPEÑO 'N' CHEESE CORNBREAD WAFFLES In a medium bowl, combine the cornmeal, flour, baking powder, salt, jalapeño peppers and cheese until well mixed.

In a separate bowl, beat the eggs. Whisk in the vegetable oil and buttermilk until thoroughly blended. Pour the wet ingredients into the cornmeal mixture, and whisk until well blended.

Continued on next page . . .

Grease and preheat the waffle iron. Add 1 to 2 cups of the batter, close the lid and cook the waffle(s) until it is brown, crisp and cooked. Transfer the cooked waffle(s) to a plate, and keep warm either in your oven or on the cool side of your grill. Repeat with the remaining waffle batter. (You should have 12 to 16 waffles.)

FINISH BURGERS Prepare your grill for direct grilling, medium heat. Line a plate with paper towels.

Place the bacon on the grill and cook until the fat starts to render and crisp. Transfer to the paper towels to drain, and set aside.

Place the burgers on the grill and cook until colour has been established, 8 to 10 minutes. Flip the burgers, and arrange 2 to 3 strips of bacon and a thick slice of cheese on each patty. Close the lid of your grill and continue to cook the burgers until the internal temperature of the meat reaches 160°F. Remove from the grill and keep warm while you finish the rest of the dish.

Preheat a skillet on your grill side-burner or on the stove. Once it is hot, add the eggs and fry, sunny side up, until the whites are set but the yolks are still runny. Remove from the heat.

TO ASSEMBLE In a small bowl, mix the mayonnaise and Slow Smoke Gold together. Smear some of the mixture on a waffle, and add a burger patty and a fried egg. Top with another waffle. Serve immediately—with a stack of napkins!

Food scientists and health inspectors tell us that raw and improperly cooked meats can cause illness. We're told to keep meats refrigerated, surfaces scrupulously clean and burgers cooked until they're well done. So, what do you do if you or one of your guests likes meat cooked below the recommended "safe" temperature? It takes a quick science lesson to know for sure.

Bacteria need two things to grow: air and time. So, the more of a meat that is exposed to air, the more surface area it provides for bacteria to grow. This explains why a whole roast contains fewer bacteria than ground meat. The roast may be bigger, but only its outside surface is exposed to air. In contrast, ground meat, which has been cut in small pieces then forced through a grinding plate, has lots of surfaces exposed to air. So when it comes to cooking burgers, consider if the meat has been exposed to air and for how long. If you are unsure of *when* the meat was ground, it is best to cook to a well-done temperature using a thermometer. If you stood at your butcher's counter and watched the staff grinding the meat right in front of you, or you ground it yourself at home and you handled and refrigerated it properly, then you can cook a burger to a perfect medium-rare, and that's perfectly okay!

VAL'S AWARD-WINNING
APPLE BURGERS

After attending a number of barbecue competitions with House of Q, my sister, Valerie Bielenda, was inspired to create a burger and asked if she should enter it in the Canadian National BBQ Championships on behalf of the team. There were 35 or so burger entries that year, and at her very first competition, Val was awarded third place for this burger. Good on you, Val!

1½ lbs ground beef

½ red bell pepper, diced

½ onion, diced

3 Granny Smith apples, unpeeled,
  1 cored and grated, 2 sliced off the core

1 Tbsp House of Q House Rub or
  your favourite barbecue seasoning

Pinch of cayenne pepper

Pinch of salt

1 lb bacon, cut in thick slices

½ to 1 cup House of Q Apple Butter
  BBQ Sauce or your favourite
  fruit-based barbecue sauce

6 to 8 very thick slices extra-aged
  cheddar cheese

6 to 8 soft white burger buns,
  toasted and cut in half

2 to 3 leaves green leaf lettuce

White Barbecue Sauce (optional, page 167)

In a large bowl, combine the ground beef, red peppers, onions, grated apples, rub, cayenne and salt. Using your hands, mix until the ingredients are evenly distributed throughout the meat.

Line a baking sheet with waxed paper or parchment paper. Divide the meat into 6 to 8 equal balls, and then form each one into a patty about ½ to ¾ inch thick. Arrange the patties on the baking sheet, and refrigerate them for 30 to 60 minutes to "set" while you clean up and prepare your grill.

Prepare your grill for direct grilling, medium heat. Place the bacon on the grill, and cook until the fat starts to render and crisp. Transfer the cooked bacon to a plate lined with paper towels, and then increase the temperature of the grill to medium-high.

Place the burgers on the grill, and sear on one side with the lid closed until a crust has formed. Place the apple slices on the grill to warm through and get some grill marks. Flip the burgers over, brush them with the Apple Butter BBQ sauce, and then top each one with a slice of grilled apple and cheese. Close the lid and cook for another 4 to 8 minutes, or until the internal temperature of the meat reaches 160°F. Remove from the grill and allow to rest for a few minutes. Slide the burgers onto individual buns, top with lettuce and bacon and a generous smear of the optional white barbecue sauce. And congratulate Val! This is an awesome burger.

PORK

PORK IS THE MOST POPULAR MEAT ON THE PLANET BECAUSE IT'S VERSATILE, EASY TO COOK AND MAKES REALLY TASTY DISHES. FOR THE BEST FLAVOUR, SEEK OUT ARTISAN PRODUCERS OR LOCAL FARMERS RAISING THE ANIMALS RIGHT IN YOUR COMMUNITY.

BEER-BRINED
PORK CHOPS

Brining pork is a great way to add flavour and moisture that reaches deep into the meat. Use a dark malty beer to add complexity to this dish. Once the chops have been brined for a few hours, add even more flavour by dusting them with a simple rub. Serve these chops with Apple Butter Onions (page 168).

BEER BRINE

2 cups water

2 cups dark beer

¼ cup kosher salt

3 Tbsp fancy molasses

Ice

4 to 6 thickly cut centre-cut
    pork loin chops

SIMPLE PORK RUB

2 Tbsp black pepper

2 tsp sea salt or kosher salt

2 tsp ground dried thyme

2 tsp granulated garlic

BEER BRINE In a large bowl, combine the water, beer, salt and molasses and stir until the salt and sugar are completely dissolved. Add ice to cool the mixture. Place the pork chops in the brine, and refrigerate for at least 2 hours.

Remove the chops from the brine, rinse with fresh water and pat dry with paper towels.

SIMPLE PORK RUB In a small bowl, combine the pepper, salt, thyme and granulated garlic until well mixed. Dust each chop on both sides with this rub.

TO FINISH Prepare your grill for indirect grilling, medium-high heat. Brush or wipe the grates with oil, if necessary. First place the chops directly over the heat, and sear them to establish the colour, create grill marks and crisp the outside of the chops. Turn them over and sear the other side, and then transfer the chops to the cool side of the grill. Cook with the lid closed, and remove from the grill when the internal temperature of the meat reaches 145°F, about another 10 minutes. Allow to rest for 5 minutes before serving.

When competition BBQ was starting to get under my skin, I wanted to master the craft of barbecue. The last thing I wanted to do was to turn out great food using someone else's commercial product. Call me stubborn, I guess, but I wanted to create my own rubs, sauces, mops, glazes, finishing spritzes and whatever else my meats seemed to need.

In the spring of 2005, I was planning to cook some pork butts, and I got it stuck in my head that apples and pork go well together. I wanted to craft an apple-based barbecue sauce that made my pulled pork really different, so I started with an off-the-shelf barbecue sauce and added applesauce. The results weren't bad, I admit. A bit of rum made it even better, and so after consulting Glenn Erho, my cookmate at the time, and our volunteer "eaters," we decided to use the sauce at our first-ever competition, the Canadian Festival of Chili and BBQ (B.C. Championship). And we won ribbons!

After several competitions using this sauce, Corinne—my spouse and, of course, head critic—suggested that to create a sauce, I couldn't just doctor something that's storebought, I needed to craft it from scratch. That fall I bought apples. I peeled, cored and simmered them with sugar, molasses, and all kinds of "apple-pie-like" spices and then puréed them with Mom's hand-me-down immersion blender. Version 1 was okay. Versions 2 through 4 were even better. So when we got to version 15 or so, the recipe was pretty consistent.

We knew that we would use quite a bit of sauce during a single competition, and thus I decided to make a big batch and can it in Mason jars. That way I could have sauce for a couple of events without having to make more each time. At least that was the plan initially. . . At our first event for the 2006 competition-BBQ season, we used this sauce in our pulled pork dish, and after we'd sent our tray to the judges, we allowed the public to sample what was left over. It seemed like no one left our table without asking, "So, where can we get this sauce? It's really good!" In jest I answered, "I have this one Mason jar left. You got five dollars?" It was my first sale, and the start of our barbecue sauce business.

AWARDS
1ST: BBQ on the Bow, Calgary, AB—2007, 2010
3RD: National BBQ Festival, Douglas, GA—2007, 2009

CRANKED-UP
MEATLOAF

You grew up on meatloaf, didn't you? I did. And I wanted to forget it for the longest time too! However, these dishes from days gone by have become popular again—and I've discovered that meatloaf prepared on the grill is fantastic, especially when it's smoked. Try this version, which I've cranked up a few notches from the one Mom used to make by adding plenty of bacon. Serve this meatloaf with Dill Smashed Potatoes (page 130) for an awesome meal.

2 lbs ground pork

1 cup medium or hot salsa

2 cups tortilla chips, crushed (I prefer multicoloured ones)

2 eggs

2 cups grated cheddar or Monterey Jack cheese

2 Tbsp House of Q House Rub or your favourite barbecue seasoning

1 lb bacon, cut in thin slices

House of Q Rock'n Red BBQ Sauce (optional, more for serving)

In a large bowl, combine the pork, salsa, tortilla chips, eggs, cheese and rub until well mixed. Turn the mixture onto a clean work surface, and using your hands, form the meat into a large loaf about 8 to 10 inches long.

Wrap the meatloaf with the bacon strips so the loose ends are underneath the loaf. (Or if you prefer, arrange the bacon in a lattice pattern on a clean work surface, set the meatloaf on top and roll the meat over the bacon, pressing the strips into the loaf to completely cover it.) Set the bacon-wrapped meatloaf on a plate, and cover it with plastic wrap. Refrigerate for an hour or more to allow the flavours to come together.

Prepare your grill (or your smoker) for indirect cooking on medium heat. Place a sheet of aluminum foil under the grate on the cool side of the grill. Remove the meatloaf from the fridge, remove the plastic wrap and place the loaf on the cool side of your grill (or smoker) and cook for 60 to 90 minutes. When the internal temperature of the meat reaches 140°F to 145°F, brush the meat with BBQ sauce if you like. Continue cooking until the meatloaf reaches 160°F and the bacon is crisp. Remove from the heat and allow to rest for a few minutes.

Slice the meatloaf into individual servings. Serve with more Rock'n Red BBQ Sauce. Thanks, Mom!

SMOKED
RIBS

Start these ribs about six hours before you plan to serve them, so they have time to cook to perfect tenderness. Try using hickory, maple or apple wood chips, which are great for pork. Serve these ribs with Grilled Corn, Black Bean and Peach Salad (page 138).

2 racks pork ribs, sides or backs

½ to ¾ cup House of Q Slow Smoke Gold BBQ Sauce or your favourite prepared mustard

2 to 3 Tbsp granulated garlic

5 to 6 Tbsp Pork Rib Rub (page 166) or House of Q House Rub

1 cup apple juice

½ cup maple syrup

¼ cup dark rum

House of Q Apple Butter BBQ Sauce, Sugar & Spice BBQ Sauce or your favourite barbecue sauce

Prepare the ribs by removing the membrane on the back. To do this, start by lifting an edge of the membrane at the end of a bone. Using a paper towel, grasp the membrane and pull to remove it from the back of ribs. Discard the membrane. Brush the back of the ribs with half of the Slow Smoke Gold (or mustard), and sprinkle them with half of the granulated garlic and then the rub. Allow them to rest for a couple of minutes, until the spices have soaked up some of the BBQ sauce. Turn the ribs over, and repeat the basting and sprinkling process on the front with the remaining BBQ sauce, garlic and rub.

Prepare your smoker or your grill for smoking, low to medium heat. If you are using a dedicated charcoal smoker start your charcoal with a small fire.

Place wood chunks on top of the charcoal, and seal up your cooker. If you are using a gas grill, create foil packets of wood chips, and preheat one side of your grill to low to medium heat. Place the foil packets on the hot side of the grill under the grate, and close the lid.

To prepare the basting sauce, thoroughly clean a squeeze bottle with soap and hot water. Rinse it well. Pour the apple juice, maple syrup and rum into the squeeze bottle, and shake until well combined. Set aside.

Place the ribs in your smoker or on the cool side of your grill, and cook for 4 to 6 hours, rotating the pork racks every hour so they cook evenly. After about 2 hours of cooking, once the surface of the meat has become dry and crusty, almost like sandpaper, spray the ribs with the basting sauce. Repeat this basting once an hour for the next 3 hours.

Check the ribs for tenderness by using the "pull test." Using only 2 fingers, lightly grasp each end of a rack of ribs and gently pull outward. If the meat starts to pull away from the bone in the centre of the rack, it's ready for glazing. If it is still tight, continue to cook it some more.

When the pork is tender enough to glaze, remove the racks from the cooker, and brush both the front and the back with the BBQ sauce. Return to the cooker and allow the glaze to set for 20 to 30 minutes. Remove from the grill, transfer to a cutting board and allow the ribs to rest for 10 to 20 minutes.

To serve, use a sharp knife to cut in between the bones. Separate into individual ribs and enjoy!

WHY IS MY MEAT SO DRY?

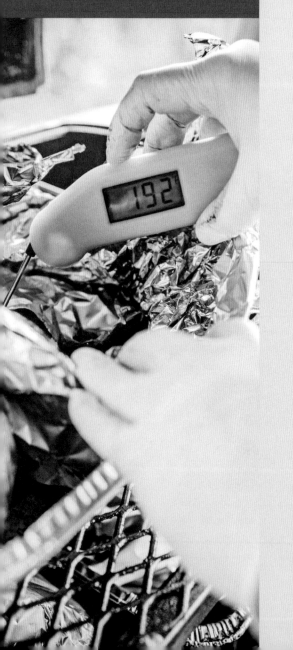

Lean cuts of meat, such as pork chops and chicken breasts, can become dry as they're cooked because they don't contain as much fat as other cuts. When this happens, it is deflating as a food experience. Who goes to a high-end restaurant and declares, "The pork chop was awesome; it was dry and flavourless"? So, what can you do to keep lean cuts of meat moist and flavourful?

1. COOK WITH THE FAT AND SKIN ON. Chicken breasts and many cuts of pork are lean meats, but cooking them with the skin on helps keep moisture inside. If you find skin and fat unappealing to eat, then remove the skin or cut off the fat after cooking.

2. USE A DIGITAL INSTANT-READ MEAT THERMOMETER. Lean pork can be served really, really juicy at a nice medium or even medium-rare temperature such as 145°F. Chicken breasts need to be cooked to 165°F. If you are guessing, you're likely to overcook meats and dry them out. So, use a thermometer and know with confidence when meats are cooked properly! Remove the guesswork.

3. BRINE OR INJECT YOUR MEATS WITH FLAVOUR. Lean meats can benefit from added moisture, and brines are a good way to do this. They add flavour and make it easier to keep the meats juicy any time, every time. See All about Brines (page 161).

MAPLE AND MUSTARD
PORK TENDERLOINS

The pork in this recipe is injected with a flavour-some combination of maple and mustard. To do this, you'll need a kitchen syringe, which is available at gourmet food stores. Alternatively, you can simply marinate the tenderloins; however, this will only apply flavour to the outside of the meat. Allow the tenderloins to infuse with the mixture for several hours before cooking them.

GRILLED PORK TENDERLOINS
2 Tbsp melted butter

2 Tbsp maple syrup

2 Tbsp House of Q Slow Smoke
    Gold BBQ Sauce or your favourite
    prepared mustard

1 to 2 Tbsp Canadian whisky

1 tsp sea salt or kosher salt

2 pork tenderloins, trimmed

3 to 4 Gala or Granny Smith apples,
    cored and sliced

APPLE BUTTER ONIONS
3 to 4 Tbsp butter

1 to 2 sweet onions, peeled and sliced

½ to 1 cup House of Q Apple Butter
    BBQ Sauce or a fruit-based barbecue sauce

GRILLED PORK TENDERLOINS In a medium bowl, combine the melted butter, maple syrup, Slow Smoke Gold, whisky and salt, and mix thoroughly until the salt is dissolved. Suck up the mixture into a clean kitchen syringe.

Place the tenderloins on a clean work surface. Carefully, inject the pork with the marinade about every inch so the flavour is spread throughout the meat. Transfer the tenderloins to a dish, cover and refrigerate for at least a couple of hours or even overnight.

APPLE BUTTER ONIONS While the pork is infusing, melt the butter in a sauté pan on medium heat. Reduce the heat to low, add the onions and cook for 15 to 30 minutes until softened. Stir in the Apple Butter BBQ sauce, and continue to simmer for another 30 to 45 minutes until the mixture is thick and has the consistency of chutney. Keep warm until ready to serve, or transfer to an airtight container and refrigerate.

FINISH PORK TENDERLOINS Prepare your grill for direct grilling, medium heat. Brush or wipe the grates with oil, if necessary. Place the pork tenderloins on the grill and sear them, rolling the loins every few minutes so they colour on all sides. Remove the pork from the grill when the internal temperature of the meat reaches 145°F. Transfer the pork to a plate and allow to rest for 5 minutes. Leave the grill on.

Arrange the apples on the grill and cook for a couple of minutes, until the fruit is softened and lined with char marks. Remove from the heat.

To serve, cut the pork tenderloin into 2-inch slices and arrange them on a platter. Set a slice of apple in between each piece of pork. Top with a dollop of the apple butter onions.

SPINACH-STUFFED
PORK CHOPS

Stuffing pork chops is easy to do and adds a lot of flavour to a meal. Serve these ones with Smoked Onion and Garlic Creamed Orzo (page 141), and your friends will think you are a superhero at the grill!

SPINACH-STUFFED PORK CHOPS
1 to 2 Tbsp butter

2 cloves garlic, minced

1 bag (about 9 oz) fresh spinach, rinsed and trimmed

¼ cup crumbled feta cheese

6 to 8 thickly cut centre-cut, boneless pork loin chops

Salt and black pepper

MUSTARD MOP
¼ cup House of Q Slow Smoke Gold BBQ Sauce or your favourite prepared mustard

3 Tbsp white sugar

2 Tbsp apple cider vinegar

SPINACH-STUFFED PORK CHOPS Melt the butter in a sauté pan on medium heat. Add the garlic and spinach and cook until just wilted, 2 to 5 minutes. Remove from the heat, transfer to a colander to drain and allow to cool to room temperature.

Place the spinach in a bowl, add the feta cheese and mix until thoroughly combined.

MUSTARD MOP In a separate bowl, combine the Slow Smoke Gold, sugar and vinegar and stir until the sugar is dissolved. Pour half of the mop sauce into another bowl (for serving) and set aside.

FINISH PORK CHOPS Set a pork chop on a clean cutting board. You want to create a pocket to hold the spinach filling. To do this, place 1 hand on top of the chop to hold it in place. Using a paring or a steak knife and holding the blade parallel to the cutting board, gently insert the tip into the chop. Using your hand as a guide on top of the chop, create an incision the width of the chop (do *not* cut all the way through the sides, or you will have a flap) and as deep as possible into the meat. I often remove the knife, insert a finger to see how well the pocket has been formed and then adjust if needed. Repeat this process with the remaining chops.

Fill each pocket with 1 to 2 tablespoons of the spinach mixture. Using your hands, squeeze and massage the filling around until it is evenly distributed inside the chop. Season the outside of the chops with salt and pepper.

Prepare your grill for indirect grilling, medium heat. Brush or wipe the grates with oil, if necessary. Place the chops directly over the heat, and sear until colour has been established on one side. Turn them over and sear the other side. Move the chops to the cool side of your grill, brush them with the mustard mop, close the lid and allow them to continue cooking. The chops are done when the internal temperature of the meat reaches 145°F. (Be careful to check the temperature of the meat rather than the filling.) Remove from the grill, allow to rest for 5 minutes and serve with the reserved mustard mop sauce.

→ *Shown here with Broccoli and Corn Salad with Sesame Dressing (page 131)*

RHUBARB-MARINATED
PORK TENDERLOINS
WITH JACK DANIEL'S APPLES

I grew up with rhubarb. Grandma had it in her garden, and the best thing she made with it was a jam that had strawberries and a lot of sugar in it. This recipe was a surprise the first time I made it, but it really is awesome!

1 to 2 lbs fresh rhubarb, rinsed and chopped

½ cup + 3 Tbsp brown sugar (divided)

3 Tbsp orange juice

1 Tbsp apple cider vinegar

2 to 3 pork tenderloins, trimmed

2 to 3 Tbsp butter

2 Granny Smith or Gala apples, peeled, cored and cut into wedges

⅓ cup bourbon or Jack Daniel's whiskey

1 tsp ground cinnamon

1 tsp ground nutmeg

In a sauté pan, combine the rhubarb, 3 tablespoons of the brown sugar, orange juice and vinegar, and simmer on medium heat for 10 to 15 minutes, or until the rhubarb is soft. Remove from the heat.

Pour half of the rhubarb mixture into a resealable plastic bag large enough to hold the tenderloins. (Reserve the remaining marinade in a bowl.) Add the pork tenderloins to the bag, seal and refrigerate for at least 2 hours or, if you can, overnight.

In a medium saucepan, melt the butter and the remaining ½ cup brown sugar on medium heat. Add the apples and simmer for about 30 minutes, until the apples are soft and a sauce has thickened. Add the bourbon (or whiskey), cinnamon and nutmeg and cook for 5 more minutes to allow the flavours to combine. Reduce the heat to low and keep warm until the pork is cooked.

Prepare your grill for direct grilling, medium-high heat. Brush or wipe the grates with oil, if necessary. Remove the tenderloins from the plastic bag and scrape off any excess marinade. Place the pork directly over the heat and sear it, rolling the meat every few minutes. Continue cooking until the internal temperature of the meat reaches 145°F. Remove the meat from the grill and allow to rest.

To serve, cut each of the tenderloins into 2-inch slices. Place 2 or 3 slices on individual plates, top with spoonfuls of the reserved marinade and serve with the Jack Daniel's apples.

BEEF

NOTHING SAYS SUMMER MORE THAN HAVING FRIENDS OVER FOR STEAKS! A NICELY GRILLED STEAK OR A PERFECTLY COOKED PRIME RIB ROAST IS A THING OF BEAUTY AND TREMENDOUSLY REWARDING TO COOK FOR BOTH YOU AND YOUR GUESTS. BEEF OFFERS VERSATILITY, FLAVOUR AND COMFORT—AND THESE ARE THE DISHES I'M MOST OFTEN ASKED TO COOK FOR FRIENDS.

PEPPER-CRUSTED
BEEF SIRLOIN
WITH CAMBOZOLA CHEESE

Sirloin is my go-to cut of steak. It is beefy in flavour and, if well aged, very juicy. If you wish, you can also make this recipe with striploin or even rib-eye steaks. See The Perfect Steak (page 64) for tips about different ways to cook steaks.

2 sirloin steaks, each 8 to 12 oz
2 to 3 Tbsp olive oil
1 to 2 Tbsp sea salt or kosher salt
1 to 2 Tbsp crushed peppercorns
4 to 6 oz crumbled Cambozola cheese

Prepare your grill for direct grilling, high heat on one side and low on the other. Brush or wipe the grates with oil, if necessary.

Remove the steaks from the fridge, and place them on a cutting board. Drizzle with the olive oil, and then generously season with salt on both sides. Spread the crushed peppercorns on a large plate, set the steaks on top and press the meat onto the peppercorns to coat it liberally. Turn over to coat the other side, and then set aside to rest for a few minutes.

Place the steaks on the hot side of the grill, close the lid and sear on one side undisturbed for 2 to 6 minutes. (Closing the lid keeps the heat inside your grill and the grate hot.) If you are seeking the perfect criss-cross grill marks, lift one edge of the steaks and check if it has established the right colour, and then lift, turn the steaks 90 degrees and set them on an *unused,* preheated part of the hot side of the grill. This is the key to creating the grill marks. Sear for another couple of minutes to create the cross-hatch marks. Turn the steaks over and sear the underside for another couple of minutes. If the steaks are thick and you have the colour you are wanting but not the right doneness, move the steaks to the cool part of your grill, close the lid and use the thermometer to check them every once in a while for doneness. A perfect medium-rare steak can be removed from the grill when the internal temperature of the meat reaches 120°F to 130°F. Allow the steaks to rest for 5 to 10 minutes before serving.

Transfer the steaks to individual plates and top with crumbled cheese.

→ *Shown here with Shaved Fennel and Onion Salad (page 139)*

SOUTHERN RUBBED
STRIP STEAKS

High-grade, well-aged beef needs only a bit of salt and pepper to bring out its flavour. However, every once in a while when you want a bit more seasoning, try this recipe. Serve the steaks with yam fries (page 101). See The Perfect Steak (page 64) for different ways to cook steaks.

1 Tbsp sea salt or kosher salt

1 tsp black pepper

1 tsp paprika

1 tsp granulated garlic

1 tsp ground dried thyme

Olive oil, for brushing

2 to 4 striploin steaks, 2 lbs total

Herb-infused olive oil or aged
    balsamic vinegar, for drizzling

Prepare your grill for direct grilling, medium-high heat on one side and low on the other. Brush or wipe the grates with oil, if necessary. In a medium bowl, stir together the salt, pepper, paprika, granulated garlic and thyme until well mixed.

Using a silicone brush, lightly brush both sides of the steaks with olive oil. Generously sprinkle the steaks with the rub mix. Place the steaks directly over the hotter side of the grill, close the lid and sear on one side undisturbed for 2 to 6 minutes. (Closing the lid keeps the heat inside your grill and the grate hot.) If you are seeking the perfect criss-cross grill marks, lift one edge of the steaks and check if it has established the right colour, and then lift, turn the steaks 90 degrees and set them on an unused part of the hot grill. Sear for another couple of minutes to create the cross-hatch marks. Turn the steaks over, move them to the cool side of the grill and cook until the internal temperature of the meat reaches 120°F to 130°F for medium-rare or 130°F to 140°F for medium. Remove from the heat, and allow your steaks to rest for 10 minutes before serving. You can cover them with aluminum foil, if you want; however, remember that they will continue to cook under the foil.

To serve, arrange the steaks on individual plates. Drizzle them with herb-infused olive oil or balsamic vinegar.

GRILLED FLANK STEAKS
WITH HERB CRUST

I was preparing for a day of filming barbecue tips for a regular segment I do on Global TV, and the menu I crafted included this flank steak recipe. I went to my local butcher to buy it, and when I reached the head of the line and asked for a flank steak, the attendant pointed to the woman beside me and said, "I just sold the last one to her." Oh no, what was I going to do? I really didn't have time to drive around to find another one. Seeing my distress, the woman smiled, mentioned that she watches our barbecue tips on TV and then offered me the steak. Her gesture saved me a lot of grief, and so somehow I feel obligated to call this recipe Christine's Stolen Flank Steak. Serve it with homemade chimichurri or your favourite grilled side dishes, such as grilled asparagus, zucchini or bell peppers.

¼ cup minced fresh parsley (dried works fine too)

1½ Tbsp granulated or minced fresh garlic

1½ Tbsp ground coriander

1 Tbsp sea salt or kosher salt

1 Tbsp black pepper

1 Tbsp crushed red pepper flakes

1 flank steak, 2 to 3 lbs

Olive oil, for brushing

Prepare your grill for direct grilling, medium heat. Brush or wipe the grates with oil, if necessary.

In a medium bowl, stir together the parsley, garlic, coriander, salt, black pepper and red pepper flakes until well mixed. Using a silicone brush, lightly brush one side of the flank steak with olive oil. Generously sprinkle the meat with half of the rub mix. Turn the steak over, brush the meat with oil and sprinkle it with the remaining rub. Place the steak directly over the heat and sear to establish a nice crust and colour. Continue to turn and cook, 5 to 10 minutes per side, and check the internal temperature of the meat. When it reaches 120°F to 130°F for a perfect medium-rare, remove it from the grill and allow it to rest for 5 minutes before carving.

Slice the steak across the grain into thin strips. Transfer to a clean plate to serve family-style, or place individual portions on each plate.

THE PERFECT STEAK
(DEPENDS ON YOUR GUESTS)

There are two paths to cooking steaks, and which one you choose is determined by how you want to serve your dish to your guests.

PICTURE-PERFECT GRILL MARKS: When you serve whole pieces of meat to your guests, grill marks are impressive. Preheat your grill to high heat, and brush or wipe the grates with oil, if necessary. Place the steak on the grate to sear the meat. Using your tongs, carefully lift the edge of the steak (being careful not to change its position) and look to see if there are good grill marks. If there are, lift the steak off the grate and turn it 90 degrees, or a quarter of a turn. Here's the key part . . . place the steak down on an *unused* part of the grill where the grates will be hot. This will sear the meat, making a second set of grill marks. Again, lift an edge of the steak using your tongs, and once the steak has been marked in perfect cross hatches, it can be turned over to finish for doneness.

PERFECTLY EVEN COLOUR FROM EDGE TO EDGE: When you serve slices of meat to your guests rather than whole pieces for each person, perfect internal colour shows off your skill. Preheat your grill to medium heat. Place the steak on the grate and sear it for about one minute. Turn the steak over and cook it for another minute. Continue this process, turning the steak over every minute or so to ensure consistent heat is applied to both sides of the meat. This process will brown or caramelize the outside of the meat while cooking the inside very evenly. When you slice the steak, it will be a consistent colour from edge to edge. This method takes a bit more practice to master, but once done properly, your guests will see that you know how to cook a great steak. This is how I most often cook steaks. I gave up on getting perfect grill marks a long time ago.

Use the following guidelines to get the perfect doneness for your steaks:

RARE (meat temperature 110°F to 120°F): At this stage, a seared steak will be *red* in the centre after being sliced.

MEDIUM-RARE (meat temperature 120°F to 130°F): At this stage, a seared steak is *pink* or just *slightly red* in the centre once sliced. Tenderloin, flank, rib-eye, sirloin or strip steak cuts are great cooked to this stage.

MEDIUM (meat temperature 130°F to 140°F): At this stage, a steak is *pink* in the centre when freshly sliced but *may turn grey* once exposed to air.

WELL DONE (meat temperature 150°F to 170°F): At this stage, a steak is *grey* throughout when sliced. Choose sirloin or strip steaks if you must cook to this doneness. Note that cooking to well done will tend to dry out steaks and make the texture more tough.

STEAK BITES

At a birthday party I was catering, I had planned to serve several tapas (small plate) dishes throughout the evening so guests could help themselves. If truth be told, this dish may originally have been intended as satay beef on skewers, but the steak got cut in cubes instead of strips that day, and these steak bites were born!

½ cup soy sauce

½ cup extra-virgin olive oil

2 Tbsp sesame oil

2 Tbsp Worcestershire sauce

4 Tbsp peeled and minced or grated fresh ginger (grated will add more flavour)

4 to 6 cloves garlic, roughly chopped

2 to 3 Tbsp sambal oelek or Sriracha (optional)

2 lbs sirloin steaks, trimmed, cut in 1-inch cubes

In a large bowl, mix the soy sauce, olive oil, sesame oil, Worcestershire sauce, ginger and garlic, and sambal oelek (or Sriracha) if using, until well combined. Place the steak cubes into a large resealable plastic bag or a glass bowl, pour the marinade over the meat and mix well to be sure the beef is completely covered. Allow to marinate at room temperature for about 1 hour, or in the refrigerator for longer. (Bring chilled marinated beef to room temperature before cooking it.)

Prepare your grill for direct grilling, medium-high heat on one side and low on the other. Brush or wipe the grates with oil, if necessary. Remove the steak pieces from the marinade, and shake off any excess liquid. (This step helps to minimize the amount of smoke and possible flare-ups from the oil in the marinade.)

Place the meat on the hotter side of the grill. If your grill is too hot and the meat starts to burn on the hot side, move the pieces to the cooler side and close the lid. Using tongs, carefully turn each piece individually so the meat sears evenly on all sides and cooks to medium-rare; this will only take a few minutes. Allow the bites to rest for 5 minutes, if you can, and serve them with skewers or fancy toothpicks so guests can pick them up.

← *Shown here with Brussels Sprout Coleslaw (page 139)*

FATHER'S DAY
PRIME RIB

A well-cooked prime rib roast is perfect for special occasions. Big pieces of meat need to be well seasoned, and I like to use seasoned salt, which is salt flavoured with ingredients such as onion, garlic and red pepper. And, if you plan to make gravy, place a foil or metal tray under the grate to catch the drippings from the roast as it cooks. The Smoke-planked Perogy Potatoes (page 132) are a perfect side dish with this recipe.

¼ cup House of Q House Rub or
   Big Beef Rub (page 165)
2 Tbsp granulated garlic
2 Tbsp seasoned salt
1 prime rib roast, bone-in, 3 to 5 lbs

Prepare your grill for indirect grilling on medium-high heat. Brush or wipe the grates with oil, if necessary. In a bowl, stir together the rub, granulated garlic and seasoned salt until well mixed. Liberally apply the seasoning all over the roast.

Place the roast directly over the heat, and sear for a few minutes on all sides to create a crust that is just shy of blackening or burning; it will soften and add flavour as it cooks. Once the crust is established, move the roast to the cool side of the grill, close the lid and reduce the temperature to medium heat. Cook for 15 to 20 minutes per pound (roughly 45 to 90 minutes total), until the internal temperature of the meat reaches 120°F to 130°F for medium-rare. You may need to rotate the roast so it cooks evenly on your grill. Remove the roast from the grill, cover with aluminum foil and allow to rest for at least 15 minutes before carving (the internal temperature of the meat will rise an additional 3°F to 8°F [2°C to 4°C] during this time).

To carve the roast, start by cutting off the bones—these can be served with the sliced meat or saved as a treat for the cook (I like eating beef ribs!). Then, slice the meat into thin slices and place on a platter. Alternately, for bigger portions, don't remove the bones; simply cut the meat between each bone. Serve immediately.

TELL ME ABOUT YOUR BEEF

Beef is one of the most popular meats but there are a surprising number of decisions to make about what to buy.

GRADE One way to get better-tasting steaks is to buy the best grade of meat you can. In Canada and the U.S., federal governments inspect our meats and give them a grade, largely based on the maturity of the animal (age) as well as the abundance of intramuscular fat. Premium cuts of beef come from animals between 18 and 30 months of age. And the best grades of beef have lots of thin streaks of fat (marbling) throughout the meat to enhance its flavour, tenderness and juiciness. In Canada, look for Prime or AAA beef, and in the U.S., look for Prime or Choice grades.

CUT Each cut of beef has its own characteristic flavours and textures; most cuts can be grilled, but knowing what techniques to use and how long to cook them is the key. Common steak cuts for searing over direct heat include sirloin, rib-eye, T-bone, tenderloin or flank steaks. However, your butcher might suggest cuts such as hanger, petite tender, flat-iron or tri-tip. The price of meats generally reflects its abundance on the animal as well as its quality, which is why tenderloin is more expensive than ribs.

AGING Refrigerating beef under controlled conditions over days or weeks develops its flavour and tenderness. (This is different from the age of the animal.) This aging process allows the natural enzymes in the meat to soften the protein strands and concentrate the flavour. Unless you buy from a butcher shop or age your own beef, it's difficult to determine how long the meat has been aged. Generally, grocery stores age beef from 7 to 14 days and only very occasionally up to 21 days. Butcher shops will often age to as much as 30 or 40 days, which makes a more tender, more beefy meat that increases the overall barbecue experience. Beef aged at home is usually wet aged, which means that the meat is vacuum sealed so there is no air and surface bacteria cannot grow. It is a process for the patient and skilled.

FINISHING What a cow is fed before it is slaughtered can dramatically affect the flavour of the meat. Once cows have been raised to a desired age, they are fed a diet that allows for a consistent fat content and flavour. *Grain-fed* cows eat corn or other grains such as barley. *Grass-fed* cows are finished on a diet of grass. I prefer the flavour of grass-fed beef. I even know of a local farmer who finishes his cows with red wine. Imagine that!

CHAR-CRUSTED
BEEF TRI-TIP

The tri-tip is part of the sirloin and is either a really big steak or a small roast. It ranges in size from one pound to three or even four pounds. Whichever way you look at it, this cut of beef is fantastic on the grill! Serve thinly sliced beef on a sandwich with your favourite toppings or more thickly sliced strips with Brussels Sprout Coleslaw (page 139).

2 to 3 Tbsp House of Q House Rub or
    your favourite beef rub

1 Tbsp black pepper

1 Tbsp brown sugar

1 beef tri-tip, 2 to 3 lbs (ask your
    butcher for this cut)

Prepare your grill for indirect grilling on high heat. Brush or wipe the grates with oil, if necessary.

In a small bowl, stir together the rub, pepper and brown sugar until well mixed. Using your hands, generously press the mixture into the meat on all sides. Place the steak directly over the heat, and sear it for a few minutes to create a nice crust from the rub. Turn the steak over and sear the other side until a crust is established all around the steak.

After creating the crust, move the steak to the cool part of your grill, close the lid and reduce the heat to low. Cook for another 20 to 40 minutes, until the internal temperature of the meat reaches 120°F to 130°F for medium-rare. (This is a steak that really warrants at most a medium doneness . . . medium-rare is best. Often I will cook this steak to between 115°F and 120°F, remove it from the grill and wrap it in aluminum foil as it rests. It will continue to cook and finish up nearly 130°F with perfect colour and moisture!) Remove from the heat and allow the steak to rest for 5 to 10 minutes before carving.

To serve, cut the beef across the grain into slices. Serve family-style as sandwiches or steaks.

BIG DOG
BEEF RIBS

Beef ribs are back ribs cut off the prime rib roast. They can be rewarding to smoke slowly for several hours on the barbecue, and the result makes the small dogs bark just like big dogs! I first prepared this recipe on Global TV with Steve Darling in the summer of 2012, and he says, "Sometimes you come across something that beats all expectations. For me, it was the Big Dog Beef Ribs. First the aroma hits you, and then you are smacked in the taste buds with flavour. Oh, so heavenly." Short ribs work well too.

1 rack beef ribs, 6 to 10 rib bones

2 to 3 Tbsp House of Q House Rub or Big Beef Rub (page 165)

1 Tbsp seasoned salt

1 Tbsp granulated garlic (optional)

2 to 4 cups beef stock

Flavourings such as soy sauce, minced ginger, garlic cloves and diced onions for the roasting pan

½ to ¾ cup House of Q Rock'n Red BBQ Sauce or your favourite tangy tomato-based barbecue sauce

Prepare your smoker or your grill for smoking, on medium heat.

Prepare the ribs by removing the membrane on the back. To do this, start by lifting an edge of the membrane at the end of a bone. Using a paper towel, grasp the membrane and pull to remove it from the back of ribs. Discard the membrane. (You can also ask your butcher to do this for you.)

In a bowl, combine the rub, seasoned salt and granulated garlic until well mixed. Sprinkle the back of the ribs with half of this mixture. Allow to rest for 5 minutes, turn the ribs over and season the front of the ribs with the remaining rub mixture.

Place a packet of wood chips, such as hickory, oak or cherry, on the hot side of the grill underneath the grate. Set the ribs on the cool side of your grill (no heat), close the lid and smoke for about 2 hours. You may need to replace the wood chip packet to continue smoking. The surface of the ribs should be dry and "crusty," which is called creating a "bark." Leave the grill on.

Pour the beef stock into a roasting pan, and add your choice of flavourings. (I often use all of the ingredients listed.) Place the ribs into the pan, meat side down, and cover with aluminum foil. Set the roasting pan back on the cool side of the grill, close the lid and cook for another hour or more. (There is no need to smoke more wood chips at this point.) To test the meat for tenderness, use a skewer or a toothpick to poke the meat. If it slides into the meat easily, almost like boiled potatoes, remove the pan from the cooker. Take out the ribs, and return them to the indirect side of the grill.

Set a sieve over a clean saucepan. Pour the pan juices through the sieve, and discard the solids. Stir the BBQ sauce into the pan juices, and bring to a boil on the stove or grill side-burner over high heat. Simmer for 5 to 10 minutes as the sauce thickens. Brush the ribs with this sauce, and continue to cook them with the lid closed until the sauce is set or caramelized, another 30 to 45 minutes. (You can brush on even more sauce while the ribs cook—it all adds flavour in the end!) Once done, remove the ribs from the grill and allow them to rest.

To serve, cut between the bones and dig in. Don't forget to bark like a big dog!

→ *Shown here with Brian's Cornbread (page 140) and BBQ Pit Beans (page 140)*

POULTRY

FOR EVERY HOT DOG AND BURGER LOVER, THERE IS ALWAYS SOMEONE EQUALLY PASSIONATE ABOUT CHICKEN OR TURKEY. TRY THESE RECIPES, AND MASTER THE SKILL OF COOKING POULTRY PERFECTLY.

CITRUS CHICKEN
WITH RASPBERRY BARBECUE SAUCE

SERVES 4 TO 6

From time to time, your favourite foods can become familiar and even tired. To help, this recipe adds fresh raspberries to a traditional barbecue sauce so it can become new once again. Start this dish a few hours before you plan to serve it so the chicken has time to marinate; you can prepare the barbecue sauce while you wait.

CITRUS CHICKEN
⅓ cup lime juice

⅓ cup orange juice

5 cloves garlic, crushed

1 chipotle pepper (from a can of peppers in adobo sauce; use more if you want to spice it up), finely chopped

1 to 2 tsp sea salt or kosher salt

1 tsp black pepper

1 Tbsp honey

2 to 3 lbs chicken pieces, bone-in and skin on

RASPBERRY BARBECUE SAUCE
1 Tbsp butter

3 to 4 cloves garlic, crushed

2 cups fresh raspberries

½ cup orange juice

¼ cup honey

¼ cup House of Q Sugar & Spice BBQ Sauce (or more for a spicier sauce) or your favourite sweet barbecue sauce

CITRUS CHICKEN In a large bowl, whisk together the lime and orange juices, garlic, chipotle pepper, salt, pepper and honey until well combined. Transfer the marinade to a resealable plastic bag or a glass container large enough to contain the chicken. Place the chicken in the marinade and refrigerate it for at least 2 hours or overnight.

RASPBERRY BARBECUE SAUCE Melt the butter in a medium saucepan on medium heat, and add the garlic. Sauté until fragrant, about 2 minutes, and then add the raspberries and the orange juice and bring to a boil. Reduce the heat to low and add the honey and the BBQ sauce. Simmer for 20 minutes, or until the sauce becomes thickened.

If you prefer a smooth barbecue sauce, strain the mixture through a fine-mesh sieve into a clean bowl. Discard any raspberry seeds or solids. For a slightly chunky sauce, just purée it, without straining it first, using an immersion blender. Or, for an even more rustic sauce, serve it as is in the pan with chunks of raspberries, seeds and all. Whichever way you choose, spoon half the sauce into a serving bowl and set aside.

FINISH CHICKEN Prepare your grill for indirect cooking on medium heat. Remove the chicken from the marinade, and place it on the cool side of the grill. Close the lid and cook for 30 to 45 minutes until the internal temperature of the meat reaches about 140°F. There is no need to turn the chicken if you are cooking indirectly. Using a silicone brush, glaze the chicken with the raspberry barbecue sauce. Continue cooking the chicken with the lid closed until it reaches 165°F. Remove from the grill and allow to rest for a few minutes.

To serve, heap the chicken onto a family-style platter, and serve with the reserved raspberry barbecue sauce.

BARBECUED CHICKEN
IN NORI WRAPS

SERVES 6 TO 8

When I first described this dish to my wife and to Glenn Erho, my cooking partner, they both had a similar reaction: "You wanna make grilled sushi?!" Well, yup. And you know what? It tastes great! Believe it or not, the hardest part about this dish is getting the rice right; the rest just follows through.

Start this dish a few hours before you plan to serve it so the chicken has a chance to absorb some flavour from the marinade; you can prepare the rice and any vegetables you'd like while you are waiting. I was told once that sushi is a celebration of texture and flavour, so choosing your fillings is where your creativity comes to play. Add whatever you like to add texture and flavour to the chicken.

BARBECUED CHICKEN ROLLS

1 cup soy sauce + more for dipping

½ cup apple cider vinegar

½ cup olive oil

3 Tbsp white sugar

2 tsp black pepper

2 Tbsp peeled and grated fresh ginger

2 cloves garlic, minced

6 to 8 boneless chicken thighs, skin on

House of Q Apple Butter BBQ Sauce or your favourite barbecue sauce, for brushing

6 to 8 sheets nori (seaweed)

1 avocado, in thin strips (optional)

3 to 4 green onions, cut in 2-inch lengths (optional)

½ cup shredded carrots (optional)

½ cup shredded daikon (optional)

¼ cup mayonnaise (optional)

Wasabi paste, to taste

SUSHI RICE

3 cups short-grain sushi rice

5 cups water

6 Tbsp rice vinegar

6 Tbsp white sugar

BARBECUED CHICKEN ROLLS In a medium bowl, whisk together the soy sauce, vinegar, olive oil, sugar, pepper, ginger and garlic. Place the chicken thighs into a resealable plastic bag or a glass bowl and pour in the marinade. Mix well to ensure that the chicken is well coated with the marinade, and refrigerate for at least 1 hour or overnight.

SUSHI RICE Place the rice in a fine-mesh strainer, and run it under cold water. Keep filling the strainer and rinsing the rice until the water runs clear. Place the rice in a large pot, add the water and bring to a boil (with the lid off) on medium heat. Reduce the heat to low, cover with the lid and simmer for 20 minutes. Remove from the heat.

In a small bowl, mix together the vinegar and sugar until the crystals are completely dissolved. Transfer the cooked rice to a wide bowl and drizzle the vinegar mixture over the top. Using a wooden spoon, gently mix the vinegar mixture into the rice as it cools. (Do not overmix or the rice will become mushy.) It will become sticky as it is coated with the sugar and vinegar, which is perfect! Cover and set aside until ready to use.

FINISH CHICKEN ROLLS Prepare your grill for direct grilling, medium-high heat, and make sure the grate is well oiled. Place the chicken on the grill, skin side down, and sear for a few minutes until the skin has established colour and started to crisp. Turn over all the pieces of chicken, and using a silicone brush, brush with the BBQ sauce. Turn the chicken over again and brush the other side with sauce. Cook until the internal temperature of the meat reaches 165°F, and then remove from the heat and set aside.

Fill a small dipping bowl with water. Arrange a sheet of nori (seaweed) on a cutting board, and then spoon 3 to 4 big tablespoons of rice along the bottom edge of the nori. Wet your hands and gently spread out the rice evenly and from edge to edge across the seaweed. Cut the chicken thigh in half lengthwise and place it along the bottom edge of the rice. Add avocado and green onions, and carrots and daikon with a squirt or two of mayonnaise if you'd like. Avoid the temptation to put too many vegetables in your roll or it will fall apart. Starting at the bottom edge of the nori, gently roll the seaweed away from you, tightly pressing the ingredients into the rice. Once the seaweed is wrapped around the chicken, keep rolling tightly and pressing gently to allow the rice to stick and the roll to come together overall. Using a sharp knife, cut the roll into 1-inch pieces. Repeat with the remaining nori, rice, chicken and vegetables.

To serve, arrange the rolls on a platter with dipping bowls of soy sauce and wasabi paste on the side.

LEMON AND HERB-CRUSTED
CHICKEN

Simple and tasty is the theme for this beautiful chicken dish that goes well with Grilled Corn, Black Bean and Peach Salad (page 138). Flattening or spatchcocking the chicken will allow for a shorter cook time.

1 whole roasting chicken, 3 to 4 lbs
¼ cup olive oil
Juice of 2 lemons
1 Tbsp sea salt or kosher salt
1 Tbsp black pepper
1 bunch fresh rosemary, minced
White Barbecue Sauce (page 167) or your
    favourite barbecue sauce, for dipping

Place the chicken, breast side up, on a solid cutting board. Using a sharp chef's knife, insert the tip of the blade inside the chicken cavity to one side of the spine and carefully press downward until you reach the cutting board. Holding the knife tip on the board, roll the knife blade downward and cut through the bones to detach the spine. Repeat this cut on the other side of the spine. Carefully finish trimming the spine, remove it from the chicken and discard. Alternately, you can use kitchen shears to cut through the bones.

Turn the chicken over and flatten the meat with your hands. This "flattening" of a chicken is called spatchcocking. Thoroughly rinse the chicken to make sure there are no bone fragments or bits that need to be removed, and pat dry with a paper towel.

In a medium bowl, whisk together the olive oil and lemon juice until well combined. In a separate small bowl, mix the salt, pepper and rosemary.

Prepare your grill for indirect cooking on medium heat. Using a silicone brush, coat all sides of the chicken with the lemon juice–olive oil mixture (reserving some for basting). Generously sprinkle the chicken with the seasoning mixture. The chicken should be well coated top and bottom with the lemon and olive oil as well as with the seasoning.

Place the chicken on the cool side of the grill meat side up and bone side down. Close the lid and roast for 30 to 45 minutes. Baste with the remaining olive oil and lemon juice while cooking. Cook with the lid closed until the internal temperature reaches 165°F in the breast meat or 175°F in the thigh or leg. Remove from the heat and allow to rest for 10 minutes.

To serve, cut the chicken into pieces, and serve with the barbecue sauce.

One of the key lessons I have learned from competition BBQ is about layering flavours. The meat is the first level; that is, the quality, trim, grade and even finishing feed can all affect the starting flavour. Next come the many options for flavour "treatments," including brines, marinades, sauces, rub, mops, glazes and finishing spritzes. For ribs and pork butts, I started initially by simply applying a dry rub; however, I soon learned from different cookbooks and other competitors to use mustard. Yes, the yellow one that you put on your hot dog. Really!

Mustard on raw meat? That seemed a foreign concept to me. So I started to experiment to see if it made a difference in flavour. And it did. It was hard to think that a thin layer of simple, concession-stand-variety prepared yellow mustard was significant after smoking a pork butt for 14 hours, but it was! The results of that experiment just fired up the creative juices and got me thinking about what flavour might be possible if the first coating on the pork was a well-crafted mustard sauce.

Mustard sauces are really common in certain areas of the U.S., but they're pretty rare in Canada. I read a few recipes to start me in the right direction and tested the first versions of Slow Smoke Gold on friends and family. Then we tested them with our competition-BBQ entries: Would the mustard sauce contribute to better competition results? It did. In fact, in 2012 and again in 2013, we entered this sauce in competition at the American Royal World Series of Barbecue in Kansas City. Among nearly 400 other sauces, it was awarded second place, twice. I love this sauce. I hope you do, too!

AWARDS

2ND: American Royal World Series of Barbecue, Kansas City, KS—2012, 2013

HOUSE OF Q
SLOW SMOKE GOLD BBQ SAUCE AND SLATHER STORY

THAI-STYLE SHRIMP-STUFFED
CHICKEN BREASTS

This recipe is based on some grilled skewers of shrimp-wrapped lemon grass that I ate at a Thai restaurant. They were wicked tasty, and I wanted to re-create that same flavour and add some chicken to the dish. Look for mango purée in the frozen juice aisle of the grocery store, or simply make your own by puréeing the rest of the mango called for in this recipe.

---

3 cloves garlic, peeled

1 Tbsp peeled and sliced fresh ginger

1 jalapeño pepper, seeded

1 lb shrimp, peeled (and deveined, if large)

3 Tbsp diced mango

3 Tbsp roughly chopped cilantro

1 Tbsp fish sauce

3 to 4 chicken breasts, bone-in and skin on

House of Q House Rub or salt and
    black pepper, for seasoning

¼ cup House of Q Sugar & Spice
    BBQ Sauce or your favourite barbecue sauce

¼ cup mango purée (thawed, if frozen)

Place the garlic, ginger and jalapeño in a food processor and pulse until roughly chopped. Add half of the shrimp, and keep pulsing until they are well mixed and you have a smooth paste. Add the remaining shrimp and pulse 1 or 2 times to roughly chop them. Transfer the filling to a medium bowl, and stir in the diced mango, cilantro and fish sauce.

Place a chicken breast, skin side up, on a cutting board. Using your fingers, loosen the skin without poking through or removing it, and place 2 to 3 tablespoons of the filling under the skin. Add enough filling to completely fill the pocket, and then smooth out the skin and the filling so no lumps are visible from the outside. Fill the remaining chicken breasts. Sprinkle the surface of the chicken breasts with the rub (or simply salt and pepper).

Prepare your grill for indirect cooking on low to medium heat. Arrange the chicken on the cool side of the grill, close the lid and cook, without opening the lid, for 30 to 50 minutes. There is no need to turn the chicken over.

While the chicken is cooking, in a small bowl, combine the BBQ sauce and mango purée, mixing well. Pour half of the mixture into a small serving bowl, and set aside.

Once the internal temperature of the chicken reaches 140°F, use a silicone brush to liberally glaze the chicken with the mango barbecue sauce. Continue cooking the chicken, with the lid closed, until the meat reaches 165°F. Remove the chicken from the grill and allow it to rest for 5 minutes.

To serve, slice through the chicken breast and bone, and place portions on individual plates. Serve with the reserved mango barbecue sauce on the side.

CRISPY CHICKEN

I love fried chicken, and this recipe is my take on an easy crispy chicken to roast on your grill. For a Southern-style dinner, serve this chicken with Mac 'n' Cheese (page 143) and dill pickles.

---

2 to 3 lbs chicken pieces, such as legs and thighs

1 small can evaporated milk or unsweetened coconut milk or 1 cup buttermilk

2 to 6 cups cornflakes cereal, crushed

3 Tbsp House of Q House Rub or your favourite barbecue seasoning

1 Tbsp sea salt or kosher salt or seasoned salt

4 to 6 Tbsp melted butter

4 to 6 Tbsp honey

Place the chicken pieces in a large resealable plastic bag or a glass bowl and add the milk. Refrigerate for at least 1 hour, or more.

Prepare your grill for indirect cooking on medium-high heat. Have ready a wire cooling rack placed on top of a baking sheet.

Place the cornflakes in a clean, dry shallow bowl. Add the rub and the salt and mix until well combined. Remove each piece of the chicken from the milk, and roll it in the cornflake mixture, making sure to coat the chicken well. Set the chicken pieces on the wire rack, and drizzle with melted butter. Transfer the rack with the chicken pieces on it onto the cool side of the grill, close the lid and cook them for 30 to 50 minutes, or until the internal temperature of the meat reaches 170°F. Remove from the grill, allow to rest for 5 minutes and drizzle with honey.

To serve, arrange the chicken on a large serving platter, and have guests help themselves. Keep lots of napkins on hand. Enjoy!

TURKEY
WITH GARLIC SCAPES

Garlic scapes are the top part of the garlic bulb that grows above the ground. They are common at local farmers' markets in the spring or late summer; if you have garlic in your garden, harvest the mild-tasting scapes instead of discarding them. Cori's Potato Salad (page 130) or Grill-roasted Brussels Sprouts (page 135) go well with this dish.

3 to 5 Tbsp soft or crumbled goat cheese

1 to 2 Tbsp House of Q Slow Smoke Gold
   BBQ Sauce or your favourite prepared mustard

2 to 3 Tbsp minced fresh oregano

3 lbs skinless, boneless turkey breast,
   sliced lengthwise into ¼- to ⅜-inch cutlets

6 to 8 fresh or pickled garlic scapes
   or asparagus, cut in 3- to 4-inch pieces

6 to 8 slices prosciutto (optional)

Extra-virgin olive oil

House of Q House Rub or salt and
   black pepper (optional)

In a small bowl, combine the goat cheese, BBQ sauce (or mustard) and oregano until well combined.

Arrange the turkey pieces in a single layer on a clean work surface. Spoon the mustard mixture onto the turkey slices, and spread it along their length. Place 2 to 3 "sticks" of scape (or asparagus) across the width of the turkey. Roll the turkey around the garlic scapes and the mustard filling. Repeat with the remaining scapes and turkey strips. (You should have 6 to 8 rolls.)

If you'd like to wrap the turkey in prosciutto, arrange the prosciutto on the work surface. Place a turkey roll at one end of each slice of prosciutto and roll it up, wrapping it around the entire roll to hold it together. (Alternatively, use skewers to hold the rolls together.) Repeat with the remaining rolls. Brush the outside of the rolls with olive oil, and if preferred, sprinkle them with salt and pepper or some barbecue rub.

Prepare your grill for indirect cooking on medium heat. Place the turkey rolls on the cool side of the grill, close the lid and cook them for 20 to 40 minutes until the internal temperature of the meat reaches 165°F. Remove from the heat and allow the rolls to rest for 5 minutes.

To serve, slice the rolls to show off their stuffing for a dramatic presentation, or simply serve them whole. Place them on a platter and hand it around.

BACON-WRAPPED
TURKEY SKEWERS

SERVES 4 TO 6

Start these turkey skewers early in the day so the meat has time to marinate before you grill it. Have ready some wooden or metal skewers, or look for more decorative, creative options such as sticks of rosemary.

---

2 to 3 cloves garlic, crushed

1 to 2 Tbsp minced fresh tarragon or savory, leaves only

¼ to ⅓ cup House of Q Slow Smoke Gold BBQ Sauce or your favourite prepared mustard

1 to 2 lbs skinless, boneless turkey thighs, cut in 1-inch cubes

1 lb bacon, cut in thin slices

In a large resealable plastic bag, combine the garlic, tarragon (or savory) and BBQ sauce (or mustard). Shake until well mixed, and then add the turkey cubes. Mix well to ensure the meat is well coated, and refrigerate for 4 to 6 hours.

Cut the bacon in half widthwise, and arrange the slices on a clean work surface. Place a turkey cube at one end of each piece of bacon. Roll the bacon around the turkey, and thread 2 or 3 pieces of wrapped turkey on each skewer for a small portion, or 5 to 6 pieces for a larger portion. Before discarding the marinade, make sure each skewer is well coated with the mustard sauce.

Prepare your grill for direct cooking, low to medium heat. Brush or wipe the grates with oil, if necessary. Place the skewers on the grill, close the lid and cook until the bacon has rendered and crisped. Turn the skewers over a couple of times to cook them evenly and give the meat some colour. The turkey is done when the meat has reached an internal temperature of 165°F, 20 to 30 minutes. Remove from the heat and allow to rest for 5 minutes.

To serve, place the skewers on a platter, or plate them individually for your guests.

WHOLE SMOKED
TURKEY

Turkey always warrants a crowd; after all, have you ever heard of a single person cooking a whole turkey to eat alone? Instead of taking over the whole oven just for the bird, use your grill to smoke it. Preparing it this way adds character to your feast. Brining your turkey first will add moisture and season the meat deep inside for added flavour.

A couple more turkey tips. I don't recommend stuffing this bird; it just adds cooking time and makes it more challenging to cook properly. Also, it may be tempting to use the drippings from the turkey as it cooks to make gravy; however, these juices will be salty from the brine and smoky from the cooking process. Of course, it could be better than you expect . . .

1 cup kosher salt
1 cup lightly packed brown sugar
16 cups water (1 gallon)
6 to 8 cups ice (or more)
1 whole turkey, 12 to 14 lbs, rinsed
¼ to ½ cup butter, melted

Before you start, make sure your turkey fits on one side of your grill with the lid closed. Some grills may not have the inside height or width to cook the bird indirectly, and your turkey will not smoke properly if this is the case.

In a large, deep canning pot, stir together the salt, sugar and water until the crystals are completely dissolved. Add the ice.

Place the turkey, breast side down, into the pot or transfer everything to a brining bag. Refrigerate the turkey for at least 1 hour per pound of meat, or a minimum of 12 to 14 hours. Be sure you keep the meat cold, which helps with the brining process and keeps your poultry safe from bacterial growth.

Remove your turkey from the brine, rinse it under cold running water and pat it dry with paper towels.

Fill a foil packet with alder, maple or cherry wood chips. Prepare your grill for indirect cooking on medium heat. Place the foil packet on the heat under the grill grate, and place a drip pan under the grate on the cool side. Set the turkey on a large baking sheet.

Using a silicone brush, coat the outside of the bird with the melted butter. Even if the butter is warm, the bird is cold from the brine and the butter may harden on the bird—that's perfect! Transfer the turkey to the cool side of the grill, close the lid and allow the smoke to fill up the cooking chamber. Cook the turkey for 30 to 45 minutes, and then rotate the bird and check to see if you need to replace the wood chips. Repeat this process for 2 to 3 hours total or until the internal temperature of the white meat is 165°F and the leg meat is 170°F. The turkey should be a nice golden brown from the melted butter and the smoking process. Remove the bird from the grill and allow it to rest, loosely covered with aluminum foil, for 30 to 45 minutes.

To carve up a whole bird, start by removing the legs. Using a sharp knife, cut the skin between the breast and leg, and then cut through the joint separating the thigh from the spine. Arrange the legs on a serving platter. Remove the wings by cutting them from the breast meat and add them to the platter. Lastly, remove the entire breast by sliding your knife along the ribcage. Once removed, cut the breast into slices and arrange them on the platter. Serve family-style.

BBQ BRIAN'S
TOP FIVE TIPS FOR GRILLING CHICKEN

1. TURN DOWN THE HEAT! There is no need to incinerate chicken, so cook it at lower temperatures. Grill chicken at no higher than medium heat.

2. GRILL INDIRECTLY. Heat your grill so that one side is on and the other side is off, meaning *no heat*. Cook the chicken on the side without heat and close the lid—just like you close your oven door. Indirect grilling will eliminate flare-ups and prevent burning.

3. STOP GUESSING. Use a thermometer and make sure to cook white meat to 165°F and dark meat to 170°F. (Forget about cooking until the "juices are running clear" and "it's not pink on the inside." Those are bad habits.)

4. GLAZE (OR APPLY SAUCE) WHEN THE CHICKEN IS ABOUT THREE-QUARTERS COOKED. When the temperature of the meat is about 140°F, apply the sauce and continue cooking until finished. Again, cooking indirectly works best.

5. LET IT REST! If you allow chicken (and all meats for that matter) a few minutes to rest, they will become juicier and more tender as they cool. That is the goal, isn't it: juicy, tender grilled chicken? Well, then, let it rest!

GRILLED DUCK BREASTS
WITH CHERRY MERLOT SAUCE

SERVES 3 TO 4

It's not very often that I get to cook this dish, but when I do, even I consider it a special meal. It's tasty, decadent and perfect if you want to feature your skills at the grill *and* your favourite red wines. I'd choose nice Zinfandels to drink with this dish or even more hearty Merlot. Serve with Smoked Onion and Garlic Creamed Orzo (page 141). Yum!

2 to 3 Tbsp butter

3 Tbsp brown sugar

1 cup cherries, pitted and cut in halves or quarters

1 cup Merlot

3 to 4 boneless duck breasts, skin on

Extra-virgin olive oil

Salt and black pepper

Melt the butter and brown sugar in a sauté pan on low to medium heat. Add the cherries and wine, and simmer until the wine has been reduced by half and the liquid starts to become thick, 30 to 45 minutes. Reduce the heat and keep warm.

Prepare your grill for direct grilling, medium-high heat. Brush or wipe the grates with oil, if necessary. Drizzle the duck breasts with olive oil and sprinkle them with salt and pepper. Place the duck directly over the heat, skin side down, and sear for 5 to 10 minutes to crisp the skin and allow the meat to get some colour. The key to perfect duck is to crisp the skin, so be patient at this point. Turn the duck over and move it to a cool part of your grill. Close the lid and cook until the internal temperature of the meat reaches 125°F to 130°F. Remove the meat from the grill and allow it to rest for 5 to 10 minutes.

To serve, cut the duck on an angle into ½-inch slices. Arrange 3 to 4 slices on individual plates. Garnish with some of the cherries, and then spoon some of the sauce on top.

SEAFOOD

WHETHER YOU'VE BOUGHT FRESH SHELLFISH FRESH OFF A FISHING BOAT OR CAUGHT THE FISH YOURSELF, GRILLING IS A GREAT WAY TO ADD CHARACTER TO SEAFOOD. RESPECT THE NATURAL FLAVOUR OF THE FISH, AND SIMPLY ENHANCE IT WITH OTHER INGREDIENTS.

SHRIMP
TACOS

This is a fantastic dish to eat outside as you entertain guests. Have all the ingredients on a big platter, and allow everyone to create their own taco. As an alternative, use lettuce leaves instead of tortillas for a low-carb or gluten-free option. Serve with ice-cold beer and chips and Grilled Tomato Salsa (page 168).

½ **cup lime juice**

½ **cup lemon juice**

2 **tsp sea salt or kosher salt**

1 **tsp ground dried ancho chili or your favourite chili powder**

2 **lbs shrimp, peeled (and deveined, if large)**

6 to 8 **small or** 3 to 4 **large flour tortillas, warmed**

1 or 2 **avocado(s), sliced**

1 **bunch fresh cilantro, stems removed and leaves roughly chopped**

½ **lb Savoy cabbage, shredded**

2 to 3 **green onions, diced**

In a small bowl, stir together the lime juice, lemon juice, salt and chili powder until well mixed. Place the shrimp in a large glass bowl or a resealable plastic bag, and add the marinade. Allow to sit at room temperature for 30 minutes or up to 1 hour.

Prepare your grill for direct grilling, medium to medium-high heat. Brush or wipe the grates with oil, if necessary. Place the shrimp directly on the grill (or thread them onto skewers if they are small), and cook until they turn pink but are still slightly grey in the centre, 2 to 4 minutes, possibly longer. Remove the shrimp from the grill and set aside.

To make the tacos, arrange a tortilla shell on your plate. Fill it with shrimp, avocado, cilantro, cabbage and green onions. Fold the tortilla in half or roll it up.

PLANKS AND
GRILL STONES

When you are cooking more delicate foods that have a tendency to come apart on the grill or even fall through the grates, such as fish or vegetables, a cooking plank or grill stone can help.

Planks are a great way to add smoky flavour to a meal and can also double as a "platter" on which to present the finished dish to your guests straight from the grill. Planks are made from wood, such as cedar, alder, oak, hickory or even maple. Those made for cooking are generally thin and unseasoned, so resist the temptation to use your neighbour's cedar fence board or a wood shingle—you really don't know what paints or coatings have been applied to that board.

Once you've selected your plank, the next thing to consider is whether to soak it or not. The idea behind planking is that as the wood smoulders, it creates smoke, which adds flavour to your dish. You want to keep the plank smouldering throughout the cooking time without it falling apart before your food is fully cooked. So, if you are cooking foods, such as a whole fish or a pork tenderloin, that might take a bit of time on the grill, soaking the plank helps to prolong the smoking time and allows the wood to last longer on the heat. Always use a new (unused) plank for each meal.

Here's another tip. When cooking with a plank, always keep a spray bottle of water at hand. If your plank gets too hot and bursts into flames, simply spritz it with water to put out the fire and keep cooking. Once the plank is wet, it is less likely to ignite again, though it will produce less smoke.

Grill stones are an alternative to wood planks. They are made of materials such as lava rock, soapstone or ceramic. Of course, these materials don't smoke like wood planks; however, once treated, they provide a fantastic non-stick cooking surface and, because they are porous, add moisture to your meals. Your chicken, fish and pork dishes will be juicier simply by using a grill stone. Treat grill stones like your mom's cast-iron pan: brush or wipe them regularly with oil, and avoid washing them with soap.

I particularly like my lava-rock grill stone because it's self-cleaning. Once I've cooked a meal on one side, I allow the stone to cool, and then simply turn it over. With the dirty side facing the flames, any food residue burns off while I'm cooking on the top side. I say brilliant!

MAPLE
SALMON

On the West Coast, we see our fair share of wild, ocean-caught salmon in stores. Like really good beef, you need only enhance the natural flavour of this fish with a few complements rather than inundating it with many strong ones. Like Mom said, keep it simple. I like sockeye or chinook salmon for this recipe, but play around with different fish and discover your own favourites.

And here's a tip. Once you've removed the fish from the grill, leave the heat on and continue to cook the fish skin until it is crispy but not burned. It will peel off the grill in one piece and is fantastic minced and used as a garnish for salad or sprinkled over the cooked salmon.

1 fresh salmon fillet, 2 to 3 lbs,
   skin on, pin bones removed

Olive oil

1 to 2 tsp sea salt or kosher salt

1 tsp ground dried chipotle pepper

2 Tbsp good-quality Canadian maple syrup

2 Tbsp balsamic vinegar

Green onions, thinly sliced for garnish

Place the salmon in a glass baking dish, and brush it lightly with olive oil. Sprinkle with the salt and chipotle pepper.

Prepare your grill for direct grilling, low to medium heat. Brush or wipe the grates with oil, if necessary. In a small bowl, whisk together the maple syrup and balsamic vinegar. Just before grilling, liberally brush the fish with half of this mixture. Reserve the remaining half for basting.

Place the salmon, skin side down, directly on the grate and close the lid. Leave the salmon in place (do not turn it). The skin will stick to the grate and prevent the flesh from overcooking. Cook for 10 to 15 minutes, and then baste the salmon with the reserved sauce, and cook it for another couple of minutes until the fish begins to flake or the internal temperature of the fish reaches 130°F.

To remove the fish, slide your grilling spatula between the crisped skin and the flesh, separating them. Gently lift the fish onto a serving platter or cutting board, but leave the skin on the grate. (Having a second person to help you do this is helpful.) Garnish the fish with green onions and serve, family-style, on the platter.

GRILLED WHOLE SALMON
WITH YOGHURT DILL SAUCE

SERVES 6 TO 10

Fresh, wild sockeye salmon has outstanding flavour all by itself—it doesn't need a whole bunch of added ingredients. If you get inspired to stuff salmon, keep in mind that you want to simply enhance the flavour and not mask it. This recipe calls for a butterflied fish (meaning that the fish is still whole but the bones have been removed); if you're not keen to do this yourself, ask your fishmonger to do it for you or use two fillets instead.

1 cup plain yoghurt

½ cup shredded cucumber

3 Tbsp chopped fresh dill
   + 1 whole bunch, unchopped

1 whole salmon, 3 to 4 lbs, head removed
   and discarded, flesh rinsed and butterflied

6 to 8 Tbsp butter, room temperature

Salt and black pepper

2 lemons, cut in slices

2 limes, cut in slices

In a small bowl, combine the yoghurt, cucumber and chopped dill. Refrigerate until well chilled.

Prepare your grill for direct grilling, low to medium heat. Brush or wipe the grates with oil, if necessary. Rub the inside of the fish with butter, and then season it with salt and pepper. Fill the cavity with the sliced lemons and limes and the unchopped dill. Using kitchen twine, tie around the fish every 3 to 4 inches to hold it together.

Place the salmon directly on the grill, close the lid and cook for 15 to 20 minutes. Using a wide spatula, gently turn the fish over and cook for another 15 to 20 minutes or until the internal temperature of the fish reaches 130°F. Gently transfer the fish to a cutting board, and using scissors, cut away and discard the kitchen twine. Remove and discard the cooked lemons, lime and dill.

To serve, cut the salmon into individual portions. Spoon the yoghurt-dill sauce in a serving bowl, and serve with the fish.

HOUSE OF Q
FISH AND CHIPS

SERVES 4 TO 6

Our House of Q competition team entered this dish in the Canadian National BBQ Championships in Whistler, B.C., in 2007. When we sent our tray in to the judges, it was presented just as you would get fish and chips in a restaurant: the fries were tucked into a newspaper cone, the fish was arranged on top with a squirt of spicy mayo to finish. The judges went for the surf and turf entry instead that year, and we finished in sixth place; however, this is still a darn tasty dish.

The terms *sweet potato* and *yam* have always been confused. For this recipe, use the sweet orange tubers rather than the starchy white ones. And serve this dish with a local microbrewery beer, such as an IPA or a malty lager.

GRILLED HALIBUT
½ cup orange juice
Juice and zest of 1 lime
¼ cup olive oil
2 serrano chilies, seeded and minced
1 to 2 cloves garlic, minced
¼ tsp paprika
1½ to 2 lbs halibut fillets, skin on,
    cut in strips 1 to 1½ inches wide

YAM FRIES
1 Tbsp minced fresh rosemary
1 Tbsp ground cumin
Kosher salt and black pepper
2 yams, cut into ⅜-inch-thick wedges or fries
2 Tbsp olive oil

CHIPOTLE MAYO
½ cup mayonnaise
1 to 2 chipotle peppers (from a can of
    peppers in adobo sauce), finely chopped

GRILLED HALIBUT In a medium bowl, whisk together the orange juice, lime juice and zest, olive oil, chilies, garlic and paprika until well mixed. Place the halibut in a large resealable plastic bag, add the marinade and mix gently to coat the fish. Refrigerate for up to 1 hour, turning the fish once.

YAM FRIES In a bowl, combine the rosemary, cumin, salt and pepper. In a separate bowl, coat the yam wedges with olive oil. Sprinkle the wedges with the spice mixture, and toss until all the pieces are well coated.

CHIPOTLE MAYO In a small bowl, mix together the mayonnaise and chipotle peppers until well combined. Cover and refrigerate until needed.

FINISH HALIBUT AND FRIES Prepare your grill for direct cooking, one side on medium-high heat and the other on medium heat. Place the halibut, skin side down, directly over the cooler side and close the lid. Cook until the fish flakes with a fork or the internal temperature of the fish reaches 130°F (about 10 to 30 minutes). If you cook the fish with the lid closed, there is no need to turn it over. (The cooking time will vary depending on the temperature of the grill and the thickness of the fillets.)

While the fish is cooking, place the yams on the hot side of the grill, and cook, turning them regularly, until they are tender and have grill marks, 5 to 10 minutes. You may be opening and closing the grill lid through this process—however, keep in mind that closing the lid helps cook the fish.

To serve, divide the yam fries among 4 to 6 individual plates, place a piece of fish on the fries and spoon a scoop of the chipotle mayo on top.

PLANKED CRAB-STUFFED
PEPPERS

I am a fan of crab cakes—at least the ones that actually have crab in them rather than a whole bunch of fillers. A good crab cake needs to have crab in it, right? Here's a variation on the usual crab cake, stuffed into bell peppers and planked for extra flavour. For tips on cooking with planks, see Planks and Grill Stones (page 96).

Serve these peppers as an appetizer, a side dish or even paired with your favourite steak as a variation on the traditional "surf and turf"! They look great on a platter nestled into a fresh market salad or a nice rice pilaf.

4 to 5 Tbsp butter

¼ cup finely diced onions

1 clove garlic, crushed

3 to 4 whole medium bell peppers or
    10 to 12 whole baby bell peppers

½ to ¾ lb cooked crabmeat, chilled
    (fresh is best, or use 2 cans of
    drained lump crabmeat)

1 to 2 Tbsp chopped fresh dill

6 to 8 Tbsp panko or regular bread crumbs

Salt and black pepper

1 cedar plank, unsoaked

Melt the butter in a sauté pan on low to medium heat. Add the onions and garlic and cook until softened, about 10 minutes. Remove from the heat and allow to cool.

Wash the whole bell peppers. Cut off one side of each pepper so you can fill the inside. Dice the portions of peppers you've removed (you'll need 3 to 4 tablespoons), and set them aside. Remove and discard the seeds and white pith.

In a clean bowl, combine the crab, sautéed onions and garlic (and pan juices), the diced bell peppers, dill and panko (or bread crumbs) until well mixed. Season to taste with salt and pepper. Stuff the bell peppers with the crab filling.

Prepare your grill for direct grilling, medium heat. Place the plank on the grill, and close the lid until you smell the plank starting to smoke (and you may hear it crackle), 5 to 10 minutes. Place the peppers on the plank, close the lid and grill-smoke them for 20 to 40 minutes depending on their size, or until the peppers are soft and cooked through.

To serve, arrange the bell peppers on a platter and pass them around.

MARINADE MYTHS

Marinades are often a mixture of an acid, such as fruit juice, soy sauce or even wine, mixed with an oil, such as olive oil, and seasoned with fragrant herbs or spices, such as garlic or ginger. There are many recipes for marinades, and there may be one that you hold sacred. Marinades are a great way to add flavour to meats and seafood, but here are two commonly held beliefs about how they work—that are actually myths.

MYTH ONE: MARINADES PENETRATE THE MEAT OR SEAFOOD TO GIVE IT FLAVOUR. Not true! They are all about applying flavour to the surface. Often the flavours are so strong that it seems like they are coming from deep inside the meat or seafood; however, unless the food has been marinated in a vacuum (called a tumbler), that's usually not the case. If you're preparing meats at home and you want the flavour to penetrate *deep* into the flesh, don't use a marinade; use a brine or inject the marinade with a syringe.

MYTH TWO: MARINADES TENDERIZE THE MEAT AS THEY FLAVOUR IT. Again, usually *not true!* The process of tenderizing meats involves the protein denaturing, softening and loosening. This can be done by physically manipulating the meat (mechanical tenderizing) or by chemical tenderizing. Many marinades, particularly those made at home, don't contain the right chemicals to properly denature a protein. However, some natural ingredients, such as pineapple, papaya and kiwi, do have enzymes that can tenderize meats.

So knowing that, it is possible to make a homemade marinade that will tenderize meats by adding pineapple juice, right? Well, sort of . . . The first challenge is to get the enzymes deep into the meat rather than just on the surface to make sure they do their job. The second challenge is to make sure the enzymes don't do their job too well, which can lead to the surface of the meat becoming overly soft and mushy—a texture that most people don't find appealing. Using pineapple, papaya or kiwi in a marinade for chicken can cause the skin on the bird to become mushy and disintegrate. Again, if you're preparing meats at home, the easiest and most foolproof way to add flavour and moisture to the *inside* of meat is by using a brine or injecting it with a syringe. Marinades are all about the *outside* of meat.

GRILLED OYSTERS
À LA HOUSE OF Q

After living on the coast of the Pacific Ocean for many years, I finally started to appreciate fresh shellfish straight from the grill. These oysters make a completely awesome appetizer for your summer wine party or if you get enough, an entrée for your meal. There are many different kinds of oysters; I like ones that are large enough to hold the toppings for this dish but can easily be eaten in one bite.

12 to 18 fresh oysters (Royal Miyagi are ideal)

3 to 4 Tbsp chili powder

½ cup butter, room temperature

3 cloves garlic, minced

1 shallot, minced

2 to 3 Tbsp panko or regular bread crumbs

1 to 2 Tbsp House of Q House Rub or
   Basic BBQ Rub (page 164)

¼ cup grated Romano cheese

1 lemon, cut into wedges

4 to 12 soft buns or a soft baguette, cut in pieces

Using a shucking tool, shuck the oysters. Separate the oysters from their shell, reserving the oysters in one bowl and the shells in another. Rinse both the oysters and the shells thoroughly under cold running water to remove any grit. Set aside.

In a small bowl, cut the chili powder into the butter until it is well mixed.

Prepare your grill for direct grilling, medium heat. Arrange the oyster half-shells on a wire cooling rack, which makes adding the oysters to and removing them from the grill really easy. Place an oyster in each half shell, and dab about ½ teaspoon of the chili butter on top. Dress with a pinch of garlic, and sprinkle with shallots, panko, rub and cheese. Finish with a squeeze of lemon. Place the wire rack on the grill, close the lid and cook the oysters for 10 to 20 minutes, or until the butter is bubbly and the cheese has melted on top of the oyster. Remove from the grill.

To serve, transfer the oysters to a serving platter and pass them around. Make sure you soak up all the butter and cheese with the nice soft buns!

BIG AL'S PLANKED
HALIBUT

SERVES 4 TO 6

Planking is a great way to use your grill and add flavour to many dishes, including fish. My dad, Al Misko, who lives in Edmonton, is an avid fisherman and this is his recipe. Start soaking the plank a couple of hours ahead of when you plan to serve the fish. For tips on cooking with planks, see Planks and Grill Stones (page 96). Make up a batch of Dill Smashed Potatoes (page 130) to go with this dish, just like Dad would, or serve with your choice of grilled vegetables.

1 alder plank, soaked in water

1 to 2 lbs skinless halibut fillets,
    cut in 1½-inch strips

Salt and black pepper

½ cup mayonnaise

3 Tbsp maple syrup or maple sugar

Soak the alder plank for a few hours. Prepare your grill for direct cooking, medium to high heat, and then place the plank on the grill, close the lid and wait until you hear the plank start to crackle like popcorn, 5 to 10 minutes.

Season the halibut with salt and pepper. In a small bowl, combine the mayonnaise and maple syrup (or maple sugar) and whisk until well mixed. Smear or dollop the mayonnaise mixture over the fish.

Arrange the halibut in a single layer on the plank, and close the lid. As the fish cooks, it will become smoky. (Don't worry too much if the plank starts to burn, but remember to keep a spray bottle of water nearby to spritz the plank if it begins to catch fire.) When the fish is firm to the touch and starts to flake and the mayo coating is nice and brown (or when the internal temperature is 130°F), about 10 to 20 minutes, place a baking sheet at the edge of the grill and slide the whole plank onto it (this will prevent it from melting a plastic surface or burning a hand, if the plank is burning underneath).

To serve, arrange a slice of fish on each plate. Spoon any remaining maple mayo into a serving bowl, and pass it around so guests can scoop some on top of their fish.

PROSCIUTTO AND BASIL-WRAPPED
PRAWNS

Although this recipe has quite a few steps to it, your guests will ultimately be impressed! The key is to start with really good-quality fresh prawns, so find a local fishmonger and get to know that person and their products. For this recipe, use peeled prawns with their heads removed but the tails still on.

Note that the wine that you use in the marinade will influence the flavour of your dish. I like to use sweeter wines, such as Riesling or Gewürztraminer. You can start the day before you plan to serve these prawns, or you can do all the steps in about three hours. Depending on the size of the prawns, have a supply of wooden or metal skewers on hand to help hold everything together.

BRINED AND MARINATED PRAWNS
½ cup sea salt or kosher salt
1 cup lightly packed brown sugar
8 cups water
2 lbs prawns, 8/10 size (meaning 8 to 10 prawns
    per pound), peeled, heads removed but tails on
½ cup olive oil
2 Tbsp white wine
3 cloves garlic, minced
2 Tbsp minced fresh parsley
½ tsp crushed red pepper flakes
16 to 20 basil leaves
8 to 10 slices prosciutto,
    cut in half lengthwise

CHILI-LIME SAUCE
½ cup lime juice
2 Tbsp white sugar
2 to 3 serrano chilies, seeded and finely diced
¼ cup olive oil
¼ cup chopped fresh cilantro
Salt and black pepper (optional)

BRINED AND MARINATED PRAWNS In a large glass bowl, combine the salt, sugar and water and stir until the salt and sugar have dissolved. Place the prawns in the brine, and refrigerate for at least 1 hour.

In a large bowl, whisk together the olive oil, wine, garlic, parsley and red pepper flakes. Once brined, transfer the prawns to a colander, rinse under cold running water and add to the marinade. Allow to sit at room temperature for 30 minutes to 1 hour.

CHILI-LIME SAUCE In a medium bowl, whisk together the lime juice, sugar and serrano chilies. Drizzle in the olive oil, whisking constantly until emulsified, and then add the cilantro. Season to taste with salt and pepper if you'd like. If you would like more heat, add more serrano chilies. Allow to rest at room temperature until the prawns are ready to eat.

FINISH PRAWNS Prepare your grill for direct grilling, medium to high heat. Brush or wipe the grates with oil, if necessary. Wrap a basil leaf around each prawn, and then wrap a strip of prosciutto around the basil leaf. If the prosciutto seems to be falling off, thread the wrapped prawns onto skewers to hold everything in place.

Place the skewers on the grill, turning them once the prawns go from grey to pink. They should be completely done in 5 to 6 minutes total. The best tip is to keep an eye on them . . . and watch for the change in colour. Look for the prawns to turn a bright white with orange bands. Be careful not to overcook them.

To serve, either keep the prawns on the skewers or remove them and place on a platter. Spoon the chili-lime sauce into a side dish, and have your guests dip their prawns in the sauce.

COMPETITION BBQ

MOST PEOPLE ARE FAMILIAR
WITH BACKYARD BARBECUE, BUT
COMPETITION BBQ REQUIRES
A WHOLE NEW LEVEL OF MAS-
TERY. IT'S THIS DESIRE TO BE
THE BEST AT WHAT WE DO THAT
LEADS PITMASTERS TO HONE
THEIR SKILLS. I HAVE HEARD TIME
AND TIME AGAIN FROM PEOPLE
EATING COMPETITION BBQ THAT
EVEN THE BEST RESTAURANTS
SEEM TO LACK FLAVOUR AND
COOKING MASTERY COMPARED
WITH MEATS BEING PREPARED
FOR JUDGING. IF YOU WANT
TO COOK LIKE A CHAMPION IN
THE BACKYARD OR TEST YOUR
SKILLS AT A BARBECUE COM-
PETITION, GIVE THESE RECIPES
A TRY. THE RECIPES IN THIS
SECTION USE A CHARCOAL OR
WOOD SMOKER; HOWEVER, YOU
CAN DO EACH OF THESE ON A
GAS GRILL USING INDIRECT HEAT
AND SOME WOOD CHIPS, WITH
PLENTY OF TIME AND PATIENCE.

WHAT IS
COMPETITION
BBQ?

Although the sport of competitive BBQ has grown dramatically in the past decade across North America, it's not uncommon for people to look puzzled or surprised when we mention that House of Q travels all over the continent to attend these judged events. If you've never attended a barbecue contest, it's worth a visit—and not just for the food!

At most contests, cooks prepare dishes in predetermined meat categories, which usually include beef brisket, pulled pork (or pork shoulder), chicken and pork ribs. Some contests, depending on the interest or wishes of the organizers or sponsors, offer additional categories. These could be broad categories such as desserts or more narrowly focused ones based on a specific ingredient such as, for example, pork tenderloin or corn.

Every team that competes brings its own barbecue smokers and cooking utensils, and there are two consistent rules across all competitions: you have to cook over wood or charcoal (no gas-fuelled cookers are allowed), and you cannot do anything to the meats before they are inspected on-site at the competition. Once the inspection is complete, you can do whatever you wish to the meats to win points from the judges.

The teams are always friendly. Everyone loves to talk about what they are doing and what gear they are using. Many teams make their smokers from scratch by doing their own welding, shaping the metal themselves and adding the unique touches that help them in their pit. It's not uncommon to bring different cookers for different meats: one device for brisket and pork, and another one for chicken and ribs. As with any competition, the cooks' priority is to win points for each of the four entries they are preparing.

To help with objectivity, the entries are "blind" to the judges, meaning that teams submit their entry in a Styrofoam takeout tray labelled with either a handwritten number or a barcode that only a scanning device will read. The judges review each tray and provide a score for presentation, texture and taste. Once the points have been tallied, the top teams in each category are determined.

Late in the afternoon, once all of the events are completed, the awards ceremony occurs. The winners for each category are announced, beginning with the lower-placing teams and ending, finally, with the top cook. Once all of the winners in each category have been awarded their prizes, the team with the most overall points in all categories is awarded the title of Grand Champion and presented with a trophy and a cash prize. In many contests, the Grand Champion can now come home after a long weekend of cooking with $5,000 to $10,000 in prize money.

House of Q has won many category awards and a number of Grand Championships. Our team has been invited to compete with the elite teams at the Jack Daniel's World Championship Invitational Barbecue, the World Food Championships, the National BBQ Festival and the American Royal World Series of Barbecue. At every one of these events, where only the top teams in the world compete, House of Q has been proud to come home with trophies and ribbons—and these are some of our most cherished awards.

CHAMPIONSHIP
SLOW-SMOKED RIBS

If there is one category in which House of Q has excelled in competition over the years, it has been ribs. We have won many first-place awards using this exact cooking technique. Master it, and you will have great ribs—quite possibly even ribs that will beat House of Q's!

Be sure you have some wood chips on hand—apple, cherry or hickory work well—and a roll of heavy-duty aluminum foil. And for variety, replace the honey and brown sugar in the foil packets with such flavours as peach, pear or apple juices; whisky or rum; or maple syrup, corn syrup or even soda pop.

BARBECUE SAUCE
1 cup lightly packed brown sugar
½ cup apple cider vinegar
½ cup House of Q Slow Smoke Gold BBQ Sauce
 (there really is no alternative!)

SLOW-SMOKED RIBS
3 racks pork ribs, sides or back
6 to 8 Tbsp House of Q Slow Smoke Gold
 BBQ Sauce or your favourite prepared mustard
½ to 1 cup House of Q House Rub or
 Pork Rib Rub (page 166)
2 cups honey
2 cups lightly packed brown sugar

BARBECUE SAUCE Place the brown sugar, cider vinegar and BBQ sauce in a medium saucepan on medium heat. Bring the mixture to a boil, stirring often, and then reduce the heat to low and allow it to thicken for about 10 minutes. Once the sugar has completely dissolved, remove the sauce from the heat and set aside. (You'll be using this sauce for basting the ribs at the end of cooking.)

SLOW-SMOKED RIBS Prepare the ribs by removing the membrane on the back. To do this, start by lifting an edge of the membrane at the end of a bone. Using a paper towel, grasp the membrane and pull to remove it from the back of the ribs. Discard the membrane. (Some butchers will do this for you; just ask when you purchase your ribs.)

Starting on the back side of the ribs and using your hands or a silicone brush, smear half the Slow Smoke Gold BBQ Sauce (or mustard) all over the ribs, and then coat them generously with the rub. Allow the ribs to sit at room temperature for 5 to 10 minutes so the rub can start to draw moisture from the meat and stick to it. If you move the ribs too soon, all of the rub will fall off. Turn the ribs over and repeat the layering of BBQ sauce (or mustard) and rub on the top side, the "presentation" side for the judges.

Prepare your smoker by lighting a small charcoal fire. Place unsoaked wood chips, such as apple, cherry or hickory, on top of the charcoal. Set the ribs in your cooker, close the lid and smoke the ribs for 90 minutes to 2 hours. This first step gives the meat a lot of flavour and sets the rub on the meat. You are ready to move on to the second step when the surface of the ribs is dry and "crusty." In competition BBQ, we call this step "establishing the bark."

Continued on next page...

Cut a large sheet of heavy-duty foil the width of one of the racks of ribs and big enough to wrap it completely. Drizzle the foil with ⅔ cup of the honey and ⅔ cup of the brown sugar. (You can be creative with what you put inside the foil pouches: the goal is simply to braise the ribs and add lots of flavour.) Place a rack of ribs, meat side down, on the foil. Loosely wrap the foil around the ribs and set aside. Repeat with the remaining ribs, honey and brown sugar. Place the wrapped ribs back on the smoker, and cook for another 45 minutes to 1 hour. This step makes the meat soft and tender. You will know that you are ready to move on to the third and final step when you lift each rack and feel for the tenderness of the meat. The racks should be pliable, and if you wanted to, you could easily fold them in half (but don't!).

There are a couple of other methods to test for tenderness. First, gently open a foil packet and loosely grasp the tip of a bone at one end of the rack in your left hand and the tip of a bone at the other end of the rack in your right hand, and then pull gently outward. If the meat looks like it is gently pulling away from the centre bones, almost as if it were ready to tear away from the bones, it is tender. Second, with experience you can simply lift a rack of ribs with a pair of tongs and feel the texture. If the meat breaks slightly in the centre of the rack and feels rather "flip-floppy" as you lift it, it is tender. If it is rigid, cook the rack longer or the meat will be tough.

Remove the ribs from the heat and carefully open the foil pouches. Pour the hot syrup from the packets into the pot of barbecue sauce and stir to combine. Remove the ribs from the foil and return them to the smoker, back side up.

Place the barbecue sauce back on the stove, and bring to a boil over medium heat, stirring frequently. Allow the sauce to cook and thicken for a few minutes.

Using a silicone brush, generously brush the ribs with the barbecue sauce, close the lid and allow the meat to cook for a few minutes. Turn the meat over after the sauce has started to thicken and stick to the back of the ribs. Brush the front of the ribs, and continue to cook for another 20 to 45 minutes. This step, called glazing, allows the sauce to set on the ribs and tighten up some of the meat so the racks don't fall apart after softening in the braising liquid. Remove the racks from the grill, and allow them to rest for 10 minutes.

To serve, cut between the bones. Arrange the ribs in your competition tray for the judges, or place them on a platter for your guests.

RUB'S FLORIDA
COCKROACH CHICKEN

SERVES 6 TO 12

House of Q was invited to the National BBQ Festival in Douglas, Georgia, in 2007 and again in 2009. At the first event, we had only a handful of competitions under our belt, and this is the recipe we made to take tenth place among 65 teams. Maybe the magic was from our top secret chicken brine, which has helped us win many competitions in the difficult chicken category. Or maybe it was the well-seasoned but long-unused Weber Smokey Mountain Cooker borrowed from Rob "Rub" Bagby of Swamp Boys BBQ in Winter Haven, Florida, that had been home to a substantial amount of rust, a frog and several cockroaches only 18 hours earlier. Thanks, Rub!

TOP SECRET CHICKEN BRINE
12 cups water

1 cup sea salt or kosher salt

1 cup lightly packed brown sugar

4 cups apple juice or cider

2 to 3 lemons, cut into wedges

1 to 2 sweet onions, peeled and cut into wedges

4 to 6 cinnamon sticks, toasted

6 to 8 cups ice (or more)

COMPETITION CHICKEN
18 chicken thighs, bone-in and skin on

4 to 6 Tbsp Chicken Rub (page 165) or House of Q House Rub

1 cup House of Q Apple Butter BBQ Sauce (there really is no alternative!)

¼ cup apple juice

TOP SECRET CHICKEN BRINE Place the water in a large stockpot. Add the salt and brown sugar and stir until dissolved. Pour in the apple juice (or cider), and mix in the lemons, onions and cinnamon sticks. Add the ice.

COMPETITION CHICKEN In competition, most teams cook thighs, and ideally, every piece should look exactly the same. To accomplish this, you may need to trim both the meat and the bones so that each piece of chicken is the same width, length and thickness. Competitive BBQ cooks then need to decide if their cook plan is to turn in crisp chicken skin or soft, easy-to-bite-through skin. If crisp, the skin can be finished over direct heat, which will crisp and caramelize the skin. If soft, which we do at competitions, the skin is removed, the fat on the underside is scraped off and then the skin is placed back on the chicken. (Go to competition-BBQ websites to learn more about this method as well as other competition-BBQ tricks.) Whichever method you choose, trim both ends of the thigh bone so that it is the same length for all of the pieces of chicken.

Place the chicken in the brine (without the skin, if you've removed it), and refrigerate for 3 to 5 hours or even overnight.

Prepare your smoker, medium heat. Place wood chips, such as maple, apple or alder, on the lit charcoal.

Continued on next page...

Combine the BBQ sauce and the apple juice in a bowl until well mixed. Using a fork or wearing insulated food gloves and using your hands, immerse each piece of chicken in the sauce, rolling it over to thoroughly coat the chicken. Return the chicken to the cooking rack. Alternatively, use a silicone brush to simply brush the sauce onto the meat.

If you want soft chicken skin, return the rack of chicken to the cooker, and continue to cook it until the glaze sets and the internal temperature reaches 165°F. If your cook plan is for crisp chicken skin, change your cooker to direct grilling, place the chicken pieces over the heat and cook until the glaze is caramelized and the skin has crisped. Cook until the internal temperature of the meat reaches 165°F. Remove the chicken from the heat and allow it to rest for 5 to 10 minutes.

To serve, choose the 6 best pieces and arrange them in your tray for the judges, or if you are on the deck out back, simply place them on a platter for your guests to enjoy.

Remove the chicken pieces from the brine, and dry them with a paper towel. Sprinkle some rub on the underside of each piece, and then turn them over. Replace the chicken skins if you chose to remove them, and position them so they are uniform. Arrange the chicken on a wire cooling rack that will fit inside your smoker. Sprinkle with rub on the top side and place the rack in your smoker, close the lid and cook for 40 to 45 minutes or until the internal temperature of the chicken reaches 135°F to 140°F. Remove the rack of chicken from the cooker.

Different regions within North America have flavour preferences for barbecue. For example, you will see more use of vinegar in the Carolinas. In Texas, often just spices are used, and any sauce is always served on the side. In Kansas City, the sauces are sweet and tomato-based. In a nutshell, though, you often hear people say that one area has a "tendency to use" a certain type of sauce or that a particular flavour "is popular in this area."

When I developed Rock'n Red BBQ Sauce, I felt that our sauce line needed a tomato-based sauce with a vinegar base, which is typically known as a "Carolina red sauce" or, with some added heat, as a "Texas red."

Getting the flavour and acidity of the vinegar right was one of the first challenges. I tried white vinegar, cider vinegar and even red wine vinegar. They all made a reasonable sauce; however, I found that a combination of white and cider vinegars tasted best. Next, I worked with the tomato paste. The challenge was to get enough tomato flavour without minimizing the tanginess of the vinegar or creating too thick a sauce. After a bit of trial and error as well as taking plenty of notes, I found the texture I was looking for. Finally, I added a mixture of spices to round out the overall flavour.

Rock'n Red is a great-tasting, all-around tomato-based BBQ sauce. We like to use this sauce on chicken, beef, pulled pork and even in cocktails. Try it in a Caesar.

HOUSE OF Q
ROCK'N RED BBQ
SAUCE STORY

COMPETITION
BRISKET

Beef brisket is the granddaddy of the competition BBQ meats. The brisket is the chest muscle of a cow, and it's a muscle that works hard and has a lot of connective tissue that needs plenty of time to cook properly. In other words, it's a tough cut of meat that takes patience—a lot of it!

There are two parts to a "whole packed" brisket: the lean portion called the "flat" and the fatty portion adjacent to the flat called the "point." Some cooks will separate the two parts before they cook them while others will cook whole briskets unseparated. The point is the section where you make "burnt ends," cubed pieces of the cooked point that are sauced and smoked further until they are nicely caramelized and melt-in-your-mouth tender. In Texas, brisket is often served as a humble sandwich on soft white bread with pickles and maybe, maybe some sliced onions. This is a state where the barbecue sauce is always served on the side.

COMPETITION BRISKET
1 whole brisket (point and flat, untrimmed), usually 10 to 14 lbs

2 cups beef stock

2 Tbsp Worcestershire sauce

½ cup House of Q Slow Smoke Gold BBQ Sauce

Soy sauce or Worcestershire sauce (your choice)

1 to 2 cups Big Beef Rub (page 165) or House of Q House Rub

BRISKET MOP
1 can (12 fl oz/355 mL) Coca-Cola

½ cup House of Q Apple Butter BBQ Sauce or a tomato-based barbecue sauce

1 Tbsp Tabasco sauce (or your favourite hot pepper sauce)

FINISHING SAUCE
1 cup House of Q Rock'n Red BBQ Sauce or your favourite tomato-based barbecue sauce

½ cup honey

½ cup cider vinegar

COMPETITION BRISKET Before you begin, you will need to trim the brisket. Look closely at the meat: one side will show more meat on it, and the other will show more fat. You will need to trim any remaining deposits of fat from the *meatier* ("flat") side. Using a sharp chef's knife (or a boning or filet knife), cut away any remaining silver skin (the thin pearly membrane), and remove any fat pockets. For the most part, rub doesn't stick to fat. In competition BBQ, the flat side is the presentation side to the judges, so you want to trim well on this side so that the rub will stick properly and look good. In contrast, on the other side (the fatty part), you want to leave enough fat to dissolve and provide moisture for the meat. I usually trim just the large pockets and the edges all around the brisket—that's it. Discard the silver skin and the trimmed fat. Turn the brisket over and move to the next step.

In a small bowl, combine the beef stock and Worcestershire sauce. This is your injection liquid. Using a kitchen syringe, inject from the top side of the brisket, staggering the injections in a pattern about 1 inch apart. One brisket will take about 2 cups of liquid.

Using your hands or a silicone brush, smear Slow Smoke Gold and soy sauce (or Worcestershire sauce) on the top side of the brisket. Generously sprinkle with the rub, and allow it to rest for 10 to 15 minutes at room temperature.

Prepare your smoker by starting a small charcoal fire. Place the brisket, meaty side up, in the cooker, and add wood chips or chunks, such as oak or hickory, on top of the charcoal. Close the lid and cook for 60 to 90 minutes per pound—or roughly 10 to 18 hours, depending on the size of the brisket, the amount of insulation on your cooker and weather factors as well. You may need to add more wood chips to your fire, so check about every 2 hours or so to keep the wood smoking.

BRISKET MOP Once the surface of the meat has become dry and crusty ("the bark has been established"), about 6 hours or more, prepare the basting liquid (the *mop*). In a medium bowl, stir together the Coca-Cola, Apple Butter BBQ sauce and Tabasco sauce. Using a silicone brush, mop the brisket once every hour to add flavour to the meat and keep it moist.

Using your meat thermometer, monitor the internal temperature of the meat as you cook. The meat will gradually rise in temperature to around 160°F after roughly 6 hours and then seemingly stop cooking. That is, the temperature will stop rising. This is called the *plateau,* and all competitive BBQ cooks experience this phenomenon. Be patient and keep cooking. Gradually, the collagen in the meat will dissolve, and the internal temperature will then start to rise again. When the internal temperature of the brisket reaches 190°F, roughly another 4 to 6 hours, start to probe the meat with a toothpick, a skewer or even a thermometer probe, and feel the tenderness of the meat. If the probe goes in somewhat tight and you need to pull a bit to remove it, then the brisket is *not* done. Keep cooking until the probe goes into and comes out of the meat easily. (This is similar to cooking potatoes until they are fork tender.) Remove the meat from the cooker, and wrap it loosely in aluminum foil. Allow the brisket to rest for 1 hour or more. (At competitions, I have let briskets rest for 4 to 6 hours before cutting them up.)

FINISHING SAUCE In a medium bowl, combine the BBQ sauce, honey and cider vinegar until well mixed.

FINISH BRISKET Remove the brisket from the foil, and turn it so the fat (point) side is up. Using a sharp knife, remove and discard as much of the fat as you can. Turn the brisket over. If you want to separate the point from the flat, look for the fat pocket between the two. Using the sharp knife, cut along the fat pocket, and then continue to trim away and discard the fat as desired.

To serve, slice the flat part of the brisket across the grain, and cut up the point into cubes. To make burnt ends, coat the chunks with sauce, and return to the cooker for another 30 to 45 minutes or until the sauce is well caramelized. Brush or soak the slices in the sauce. At competitions, we place slices of flat and at least 6 cubes of burnt ends in our box for the judges. At home, arrange the meat on a platter, pour the finishing sauce all over the brisket and enjoy.

PULLED
PORK

Creating competition-quality pulled pork takes patience—sometimes 12 hours or more to cook in a smoker—but the results are worth the wait. I'd argue that pulled pork is the meat first-time competition-BBQ cooks want to practise making because it's just so good! At home, serve this pulled pork on soft buns with Southern Slaw (page 138) and, of course, plenty of House of Q Apple Butter or Sugar & Spice BBQ Sauce.

1½ cups apple juice

1 Tbsp sea salt or kosher salt

1 Tbsp Worcestershire sauce

1 Tbsp soy sauce

1 pork butt roast (or pork shoulder),
    8 to 10 lbs (either bone-in or boneless)

½ to 1 cup yellow mustard or House of Q
    Slow Smoke Gold BBQ Sauce

2 to 6 Tbsp granulated garlic

1 to 2 cups Pork Crust (page 166)
    or House of Q House Rub

House of Q Apple Butter BBQ Sauce
    or your favourite barbecue sauce

8 to 12 soft white buns (optional)

Prepare your smoker by lighting a small charcoal fire. Place wood chips, such as hickory or cherry, on top of the lit charcoal.

In a small bowl, prepare the injection liquid by combining the apple juice and salt until the salt is completely dissolved. Stir in the Worcestershire sauce and soy sauce. Suck the mixture into a clean kitchen syringe, and then inject the pork butt, staggering the injections about 1 inch apart.

Using your hands or a silicone brush, smear half of the mustard (or Slow Smoke Gold) over the fatty side of the pork, and then sprinkle it with half of the granulated garlic and half of the rub. Allow the mixture to rest for a few minutes until the spices have started to absorb some of the moisture from the mustard. Turn the pork over to the meaty side, and repeat the layering with the mustard (or Slow Smoke Gold), granulated garlic and rub. Allow the rub to "set" on the pork for 5 to 10 minutes before placing it in your cooker.

Place the roast, meat side up, in your smoker, and smoke for 60 to 90 minutes per pound, or roughly 8 to 12 hours in total, possibly longer. For the first few hours, check that there is still enough wood to add smoke to your cooker—add more, if needed. Depending on the flow of air and heat within your cooker, you may need to rotate the roast every few hours while it cooks.

Using your meat thermometer, monitor the internal temperature of the meat as you cook. The meat will gradually rise in temperature to 160°F to 170°F after 4 to 6 hours and then seemingly stop cooking. That is, the temperature will stop rising. This is called the *plateau,* and all competitive BBQ cooks experience this phenomenon. Be patient. You may want to wrap the pork butt in aluminum foil to help get across this plateau, but allow it to keep cooking. When the internal temperature reaches above 195°F, the pork is done. Remove it from the heat, place it on a baking sheet or in a roasting pan to catch the juices that will be released and allow it to rest for 1 hour or more.

To shred the meat, use 2 forks or a pair of tongs, or wear food-grade insulated gloves and pull the meat apart with your hands. Place the shredded pork in a large bowl as you work. Look for and discard any undissolved fat pockets or other unattractive parts that you don't want to eat. Once the meat has been shredded, add in the pan juices and the Apple Butter BBQ sauce, and mix thoroughly while it is still warm.

There are many ways to present pulled pork in a competition tray, and you will have to create your masterpiece after practising a bit. We usually include in our tray pulled pork, slices and a few chunks that show the smoke ring, the bark and moisture of the meat.

If you are serving this recipe at home, mound the warm pulled pork on soft white buns, top with coleslaw and pass the sandwiches around with lots of sauce!

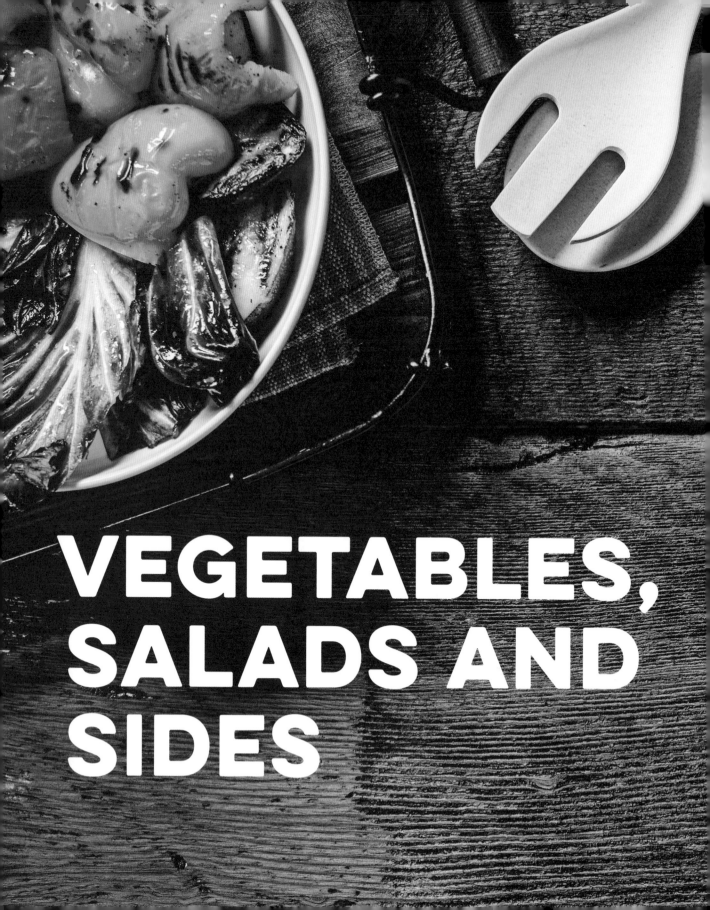

VEGETABLES, SALADS AND SIDES

MOM ALWAYS SAID, "EAT YOUR VEGETABLES!" AND SO, WE DO... WITH A SMILE ON OUR FACE. BUT WHAT'S A BBQ MEAL WITHOUT A SIDE DISH?

DILL SMASHED
POTATOES

Garden fresh potatoes with Grandma's dill are a family tradition at my house. This side dish is simple and insanely yummy!

2 lbs small white nugget potatoes
½ cup butter
2 to 4 Tbsp sea salt or kosher salt
¼ cup chopped fresh dill

Place the potatoes in a large pot of salted water, bring to a boil and cook for about 15 minutes, or until fork tender. Drain the potatoes, add the butter, salt and dill and cover with the lid until the butter has melted. Holding the lid firmly in place with a tea towel, vigorously shake the pot to break the potatoes apart and to mix them with the dill and butter. Remove the lid, and stir the potatoes to coat them thoroughly and to check that all of the potatoes are broken. Season with salt as needed.

CORI'S
POTATO SALAD

Corinne is my wife, and I affectionately call her Cori. This is one of her salads, which she created with the expertise of her mother, Lottie Kraus. Serve this potato salad cold with anything that needs a starch as a side dish. I like it best with fried chicken, like the Grill-fried Crispy Chicken (page 84).

5 lbs white potatoes, peeled
1 cup mayonnaise
⅔ cup buttermilk
¼ cup House of Q Slow Smoke Gold BBQ Sauce
   or your favourite prepared mustard
Salt and black pepper
2 red bell peppers, diced

3 to 4 Tbsp roughly chopped fresh cilantro or parsley
3 green onions, thinly sliced

Bring the potatoes to a boil in a large pot of salted water on medium heat. Cook until bite-tender (not too soft), 15 to 30 minutes. Drain and rinse the potatoes, and allow them to cool to room temperature. Cut the potatoes into bite-sized pieces, and place them in a large salad bowl.

In a medium bowl, combine the mayonnaise, buttermilk and BBQ sauce (or mustard) until well mixed. Pour this mixture over the potatoes and toss well. Season with salt and pepper, and then add the bell peppers and cilantro (or parsley). Season to taste once more, scatter the green onions on top and refrigerate for at least 2 hours or overnight.

BROCCOLI AND CORN SALAD
WITH SESAME DRESSING

This salad was created a summer or two ago and has since been added to many meals as a side dish. It is refreshing, tasty and easy to prepare. The tasty sesame dressing keeps well refrigerated in an airtight container, if you have leftovers.

BROCCOLI AND CORN SALAD
3 to 4 ears fresh corn, shucked,
    or 2 large cans corn kernels,
    drained and rinsed
1½ to 2 lbs broccoli florets, cut in
    bite-sized pieces (about 3 small heads)
½ medium red onion, diced
1 bunch fresh cilantro, roughly chopped
Sesame seeds, lightly toasted

SESAME DRESSING
1 cup mayonnaise
¾ cup rice vinegar
2 Tbsp mirin
2 to 3 Tbsp soy sauce
⅓ cup white sugar
1 to 2 Tbsp sesame oil

BROCCOLI AND CORN SALAD If you are using fresh corn, prepare your grill for direct grilling, medium-high heat. Place the corn on the grill, turning the cobs every few minutes, for 10 to 20 minutes, or until the kernels have colour and have started to separate from each other (an easy sign that the corn is cooked). Remove the corn from the grill and allow the cobs to cool.

SESAME DRESSING In a large bowl, whisk together all the ingredients until well mixed. Adjust the flavour with more sesame oil or soy sauce, if needed.

FINISH SALAD Cut the kernels from the cobs. In a large salad bowl, combine the corn, broccoli, red onions and cilantro.

Pour the sesame dressing over the vegetables, stir to coat well, cover and refrigerate until ready to eat. Just before serving, stir well again and garnish with the sesame seeds. Serve family-style.

Shown on page 55.

SMOKE-PLANKED
PEROGY POTATOES

If you really know your perogies, top these potatoes with sour cream and sautéed onions. Yum! Have a wooden plank on hand to cook these potatoes. (For tips on cooking with planks, see Planks and Grill Stones on page 96.)

3 large russet potatoes, washed and scrubbed
¼ cup butter
½ sweet onion, diced
1 cup cottage cheese
2 cups grated cheddar cheese
2 Tbsp sea salt or kosher salt
1 wooden plank, unsoaked
6 to 8 slices bacon, fried until crisp, cooled and crumbled
Sour cream (optional)

Prepare your grill for indirect cooking on medium heat. Place the potatoes on the cool side of the grill, and roast them for 40 to 60 minutes, or until a knife or toothpick can pierce the potatoes and easily be removed. Take the potatoes off the heat, and allow them to cool until they are easy to handle.

Cut the potatoes in half lengthwise. Using a spoon, scoop out the flesh, leaving enough attached to the skin so the potato has some structure. Place the potato flesh in a large bowl.

Melt the butter in a sauté pan on low to medium heat. Add the onions and cook until softened, 5 to 15 minutes. Using a fork, stir the onions into the potato filling, and then mash the potatoes. Add the cottage and cheddar cheeses and salt and mix thoroughly. Adjust the seasoning, as necessary. Scoop this filling into the reserved potato skins. (You can make the potatoes ahead to this point, and then chill them until you're ready to finish them at your cookout.)

Prepare your grill for cooking on medium heat. Set the plank on the grill and set the stuffed potatoes on top. Close the lid and plank-roast the potatoes for 20 to 30 minutes. Remove them from the heat once they are heated through and the cheese is melted. Serve on individual plates and garnish with bacon bits and sour cream (if using).

GRILL-ROASTED
BRUSSELS SPROUTS
WITH WARM MUSTARD AND BACON VINAIGRETTE

SERVES 3 TO 6

It seems that with Brussels sprouts you either seek them high and low or are so repulsed that chewing on carpet is more appealing. This recipe entices both sprout lovers and haters, so serve these at Thanksgiving and your family will love you for it! Or serve them with any poultry or beef dish that warrants an earthy vegetable. If you're in a hurry, you can also cook these sprouts on a baking sheet in the oven.

2 lbs Brussels sprouts, rinsed, stems trimmed and outer leaves discarded

3 to 4 Tbsp olive oil

Salt and black pepper

½ lb bacon, diced

3 to 4 Tbsp House of Q Slow Smoke Gold BBQ Sauce or your favourite prepared mustard

2 to 3 Tbsp Champagne vinegar or apple cider vinegar

Prepare your grill for direct cooking, low to medium heat. Place the sprouts in a large bowl, drizzle them with olive oil and season with salt and pepper. Toss gently to combine, and then place them on the grill, close the lid and cook for 30 to 40 minutes, turning the sprouts occasionally. Remove from the grill and set aside.

Line a plate with paper towels. In a large sauté pan or skillet, brown the bacon on low to medium heat until the fat is rendered and the meat is starting to crisp. Using a slotted spoon, transfer the cooked bacon to the plate. Do not pour off the bacon fat. Reduce the heat to low.

To the pan, add the BBQ sauce (or mustard), and then stir in the vinegar. Mix well until the sauce is heated through and has started to thicken. Add the bacon to the sauce and then the grilled Brussels sprouts. Stir well to coat and transfer to a bowl. To serve, arrange the Brussels sprouts in a serving dish and dig in!

GRILLED
ASPARAGUS TART

SERVES 4 TO 6

You can cook pastry on your grill? Why, yes, you can... Use a grill stone if you have one, and watch the temperature carefully or the pastry will burn. As an alternative, you can cook this tart in the oven. It is awesome served with a salad or even better with grilled vegetables.

1 sheet frozen puff pastry, thawed,
   10 to 12 inches square
6 to 8 oz grated Gruyère, Jarlsberg
   or other firm cheese
½ to ¾ lb asparagus, trimmed
Olive oil, for drizzling
Salt and black pepper

Prepare your grill for direct grilling, medium heat. Place your grill stone on the grates and close the lid.

Unroll the puff pastry, reserving the parchment paper it is rolled in, onto a cutting board or a rimless cookie sheet. Using a paring knife, score the pastry about ½ inch in from the edge all the way around to make a "picture frame." Do not cut through the pastry. Poke some holes in the centre of the pastry with a fork so that moisture can be released as it cooks. (You will end up with a flat section in the middle while the edges puff up.) Slide the pastry and parchment onto the grill stone. Close the lid and cook the pastry for 8 to 10 minutes, watching carefully so you don't overcook it, until it is puffy and starting to brown. Remove the pastry from the heat by sliding it onto the cookie sheet, but leave the grill on.

Spread the cheese evenly across the centre of the tart. Arrange the uncooked asparagus on top, placing the spears side by side but alternating the tips and tails at either end. Drizzle with olive oil and season with salt and pepper. Place the tart back on the grill stone, close the lid and cook for another 8 to 15 minutes. Check the tart every few minutes to be sure the cheese is melting and thus the asparagus is cooking and that the pastry is browning and not burning. Rotate the pastry on the parchment as needed. Once the cheese is melted and the tart is cooked, remove it from the heat and allow it to cool to room temperature.

To serve, cut into 4-inch squares and serve on a platter.

GRILLED CORN, BLACK BEAN AND PEACH
SALAD

This salad is awesome with chicken, pork or steaks, or with burgers.

½ cup extra-virgin olive oil

2 Tbsp apple cider vinegar

Juice of 2 limes

3 to 4 ears fresh corn, shucked, or 2 large cans corn kernels, drained and rinsed

1 large can black beans, drained and rinsed

2 or more fresh freestone peaches, diced

1 red onion, diced

1 red bell pepper, diced

1 bunch fresh cilantro, roughly chopped

Salt and black pepper

In a stainless steel bowl, whisk together the olive oil, cider vinegar and lime juice.

If you are using fresh corn, prepare your grill for direct grilling, medium-high heat. Place the corn on the grill, turning the cobs every few minutes, for 10 to 20 minutes, or until the kernels have colour and have started to separate from each other (an easy sign that the corn is cooked). Remove the corn from the grill and allow the cobs to cool. Cut the kernels from the cobs.

In a salad bowl, toss the corn, black beans, peaches, onions, bell peppers and cilantro. Pour the dressing over the salad and mix thoroughly. Season to taste with salt and pepper. Refrigerate until ready to serve. Serve family-style.

SOUTHERN
SLAW

Perfect with pulled pork sandwiches, where the crunch of the cabbage and the creaminess of the dressing contrast with the smoked pork. Serve with chicken or pork, or as a side dish at a picnic. Dress coleslaw within one hour of serving so the cabbage keeps its crunch.

1½ cups mayonnaise

½ cup apple cider vinegar

⅓ cup white sugar

2 to 3 lbs mixed shredded Savoy, red and/or green cabbage

1 to 2 lbs shredded carrots (optional)

1 cup sunflower or pumpkin seeds, toasted

In a bowl, whisk together the mayonnaise, cider vinegar and sugar until the sugar has dissolved. Refrigerate the dressing in an airtight container until needed.

In a large salad bowl, toss together the cabbage and carrots. Add half of the dressing and toss until well combined. Allow to sit for a few minutes. (It might seem like there isn't enough dressing, but wait a few minutes and the vinegar and sugar will soften and moisten the vegetables.) If needed, add a bit more dressing, but avoid overdressing the slaw or you will end up with a wet, sloppy mess of vegetables. Serve family-style.

BRUSSELS SPROUT
COLESLAW

SERVES 6 TO 8

During the 2010 Winter Olympics, I was a guest chef at an event for international media. One of the beef dishes I created for the guests used this salad as a topping, but it's fantastic as a side dish too.

1 to 2 small red onions

2 lbs Brussels sprouts, stems trimmed and outer leaves discarded

¾ cup mayonnaise

¼ to ½ cup prepared horseradish, or to taste

¾ cup House of Q Slow Smoke Gold BBQ Sauce or your favourite prepared mustard

½ cup apple cider vinegar

Salt and black pepper

Lemon juice, to taste

Shown on page 66.

Pumpkin seeds, toasted (optional)
Dried cranberries (optional)

Using a food processor, a mandolin or a sharp knife, thinly slice the red onions and Brussels sprouts. Place the vegetables in a large salad bowl, and mix thoroughly.

In a medium bowl, whisk together the mayonnaise, horseradish, BBQ sauce (or mustard) and cider vinegar. Season to taste with salt, pepper and a sprinkle of lemon juice.

Pour the dressing over the vegetables and toss until well mixed. Refrigerate for 1 hour or more to allow the sprouts to soften. Just before serving, toss again to coat well. For contrast, sprinkle with pumpkin seeds and/or dried cranberries to taste if you like. Serve family-style.

SHAVED FENNEL AND ONION
SALAD

SERVES 2 TO 4

Serve this salad as a side dish, or use it as a topping on Cheese-stuffed Bacon-wrapped Hot Dogs (page 35).

2 red onions, peeled

2 fennel bulbs, rinsed and patted dry

¾ cup olive oil

¼ cup balsamic vinegar (white balsamic works best, but apple cider vinegar is good too)

2 tsp House of Q Slow Smoke Gold BBQ Sauce or Dijon mustard

½ tsp minced fresh herbs, such as thyme, savory or basil

Shown on page 61.

Using a sharp knife or a mandolin, very thinly slice the onions and fennel. Place the vegetables in a medium bowl, tossing them and breaking apart the rings so they are evenly mixed.

In a large salad bowl, whisk together the olive oil, balsamic vinegar, BBQ sauce and herbs. Add the onions and fennel to the dressing and mix well. Refrigerate until ready to use. Serve family-style.

BBQ PIT
BEANS

Cook this side inside your smoker while you prepare other dishes . . . or it works just as well in your oven. For more heat, just add hot sauce to the mix.

2 to 3 Tbsp vegetable oil

1 medium onion, diced

1 Tbsp sea salt or kosher salt

2 to 4 cans brown beans, or a mix of your favourite beans, drained and rinsed (about 4 cups in total)

½ cup molasses (blackstrap is preferred but any kind will do)

2 Tbsp House of Q House Rub or your favourite barbecue seasoning

1 Tbsp Worcestershire sauce

½ to 1 cup House of Q Apple Butter BBQ Sauce or Sugar and Spice BBQ Sauce or your favourite barbecue sauce

2 to 3 Tbsp tomato paste

Prepare your smoker or your grill for smoking, on low to medium heat. On your stovetop or your grill side-burner, place a Dutch oven or a roasting pan on low heat and pour in the oil. Add the onions and salt, and sauté until the onions are soft. Stir in the beans, molasses, rub, Worcestershire sauce, BBQ sauce and tomato paste, and mix thoroughly. Place in your smoker uncovered, and smoke for 1 to 2 hours, stirring occasionally. Once the sauce has become hot and thick, either cover the beans and continue to cook, or remove them from the smoker and serve.

BRIAN'S
CORNBREAD

Many grilled dishes need a piece of bread to soak up some of the drippings or to scrape up the goodness left on a plate, which is exactly the job for a chunk of cornbread.

Butter, for greasing the skillet or pan

1 cup cornmeal

1 cup all-purpose flour

1 medium onion, finely chopped

1 Tbsp baking powder

2 tsp sea salt or kosher salt

4 large eggs

½ cup vegetable oil

1 cup buttermilk

1 large can creamed corn

Prepare your grill for indirect cooking on medium heat. Grease a 9- or 10-inch cast-iron skillet or baking pan. In a medium bowl, mix the cornmeal, flour, onion, baking powder and salt until well combined.

In another large bowl, beat the eggs. Whisk in the vegetable oil and the buttermilk. Add the creamed corn and whisk or blend thoroughly. Add the dry ingredients and mix until just combined. Pour into the skillet and bake on your grill with the lid closed for 45 minutes, or until the top is golden brown. Insert a toothpick into the cornbread, and if it comes out clean, it is done.

Remove from the heat and allow to cool. Cut into squares and serve.

SMOKED ONION AND GARLIC
CREAMED ORZO

When your smoker is going and you have a little bit of extra room, throw on a couple of onions and heads of garlic. This is just one of the possible dishes you can make with them, so be creative and come up with others of your own. Orzo is a small pasta that looks like rice and works well with this creamy sauce; however, use any tiny pasta that you have on hand.

1 head of garlic

1 onion

2 Tbsp olive oil

1½ cups half-and-half cream

2 cups cooked orzo

Salt and black pepper

Prepare your smoker or your grill for smoking, medium heat. Cut a large sheet of aluminum foil.

Using a sharp knife, cut off the pointed top of the garlic head to expose the cloves. Peel and discard any loose outer skin. Do the same with the onion. Place the garlic and onion on the foil, gathering it around the base of the vegetables so they cannot roll around. Leave the tops exposed, drizzle them with olive oil and place them on the cool side of your grill. Close the lid and cook for 35 to 45 minutes, until soft and cooked through, and then remove from the grill and allow to cool.

Squeeze the soft garlic flesh onto a clean cutting board. Remove the peel of the onion. Finely chop the garlic and onions.

Heat the olive oil in a sauté pan on medium heat. Add the garlic and onions and cook until heated through. Pour in the cream, and then stir in the cooked orzo and cook until the mixture begins to reduce and thicken, about 10 minutes. Transfer to a serving dish and serve family-style.

← *Both recipes on facing page are shown on page 73.*

MAC 'N' CHEESE

Impress your guests with this smoked version of a traditional mac 'n' cheese. It has all the creaminess and comfort of the classic dish but with a nice outdoor-cooked twist.

½ lb bacon, chopped

½ cup butter

½ onion, finely chopped

1 clove garlic, chopped

2 to 3 Tbsp all-purpose flour

3 cups whole milk

Salt and black pepper

2 to 3 cups grated aged cheddar cheese

1 to 2 lbs macaroni or your favourite
    small, curly pasta

2 cups grated jalapeño (pepper) Jack cheese

1 cup grated Parmesan cheese

Line a plate with paper towels. Place the bacon in a sauté pan, and cook on low to medium heat until crisp but not overcooked. Using a slotted spoon, transfer the bacon bits to the plate to drain. Pour 1 to 2 tablespoons of the bacon fat into a clean sauté pan, and reserve the rest for another use.

Heat the bacon fat on medium heat. Add the butter and onions, and cook, stirring often, until the onions are soft but not brown. Add the garlic and stir until it releases its flavour. Add the flour, stirring the mixture until it comes together. Cook this roux for a couple of minutes so your mac 'n' cheese does not taste like raw flour. Slowly add the milk to the roux, 1 cup at a time, mixing well after each addition so there are no chunks of flour and the mixture becomes creamy. Once the liquid has become warm, mix in the cheddar cheese. Remove from the heat and cover to keep warm.

Bring a large pot of salted water to a boil. Add the macaroni and cook according to the directions on the package, slightly undercooking it so it will absorb some of the cheese mixture and make the dish extra tasty. Drain the pasta and mix it into the cheese sauce. Stir well.

Prepare your smoker or your grill for smoking, medium heat. Pour half of the mac 'n' cheese into a large baking dish. Smother it with half of the jalapeño Jack cheese, and then cover it with the remaining mac 'n' cheese. Top with the remaining jalapeño Jack cheese, the Parmesan and the bacon bits. Smoke on the indirect side of your grill with the lid closed for 20 to 30 minutes, until the mixture is bubbly and the top is slightly browned. Remove from the heat and allow to cool slightly before serving, if you can make it that long!

Serve this dish family-style from the baking dish.

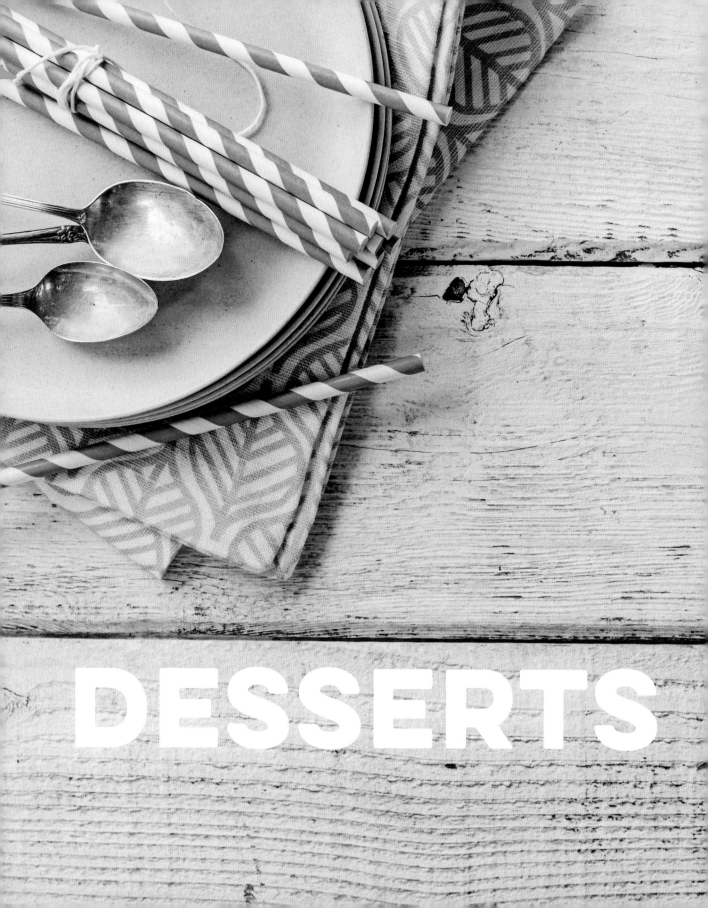

DESSERTS

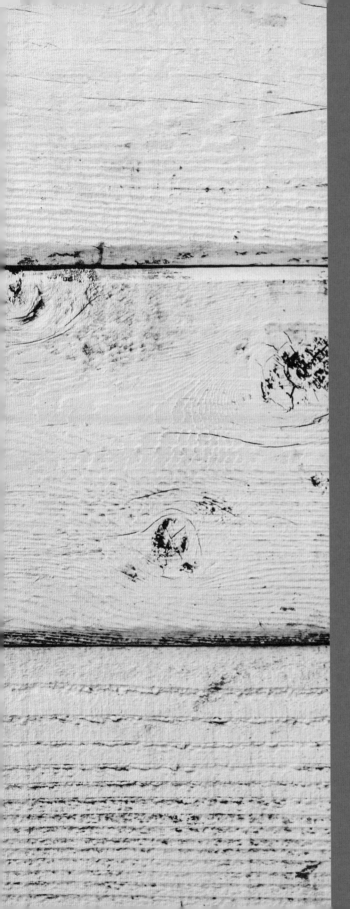

BALANCE A GREAT SAVOURY GRILLED MEAL WITH A PERFECT, SWEET FINISH. TO GET YOU GOING, START WITH GRILLED FRUIT, LIKE PINEAPPLE OR PEARS, OR LOOK TO DESSERTS THAT MOM MADE, AND THEN BE CREATIVE AND ADAPT THEM FOR THE GRILL. FEEL FREE TO DO THE SAME WITH YOUR OWN FAMILY FAVOURITES.

WRITE IT
DOWN

You may be happy to follow the recipes in this book exactly, but the best way to become a great cook is to get comfortable experimenting. Whether you are cooking for your in-laws or the neighbours or practising for a BBQ competition, I'd encourage you to take risks. If you read a recipe and think that you'd like try it with a different ingredient, give it a go. Or if you make a dish and feel that it would be even better with more of one spice and less of another, see what happens if you follow your palate. That is how you learn. You can try new ingredients, change spices, add more sauce or even try a new cooking technique . . . but keep a note of what you did.

Early on, and still to this day, I write out recipes that I craft in the kitchen. I jot down not only what I did, but most importantly the result: What did I like? What needed improvement? What spices needed adjustment? I also record what my "eaters" say after they try a dish, which helps me to improve. Family and friends are perfect testers; most people like to eat, and their honest feed-back will make you a better cook.

What I have learned is to make small changes when I'm trying to create or improve a dish. It is really easy to change three or four things at once, but then it's hard to know what contributed to a better or worse result. If you think the dish needed a bit more salt, then change only the amount of salt until you get that part right. Then work on the next improvement: the texture or another fla-vour or some other variation. Just don't forget to write it all down!

GRANOLA-STUFFED
APPLES

These stuffed apples are easy to make, and if you serve them with ice cream, they are a real crowd-pleaser.

**4 to 6 apples (I like Cameo, Gala or
   Granny Smith, but use your favourite)**

1 cup granola

1 cup lightly packed brown sugar

½ cup all-purpose flour

1 tsp ground cinnamon

1 tsp Chinese 5-spice powder (optional)

¼ cup butter, room temperature

1 tsp vanilla extract

Prepare your grill for indirect cooking on medium heat. Using a paring knife or a melon baller, create a "bowl" inside each apple by starting at the top and removing the core. Scoop out a bit more than just the core so you have a nice-sized space to fill with the granola.

In a medium bowl, mix together the granola, brown sugar, flour, cinnamon and 5-spice powder until well combined. Add the butter and vanilla and stir until thoroughly mixed. Divide the mixture evenly among the apples, tightly filling the cavity and mounding the extra on the top. Arrange the apples in a roasting pan, a casserole dish or in muffin tins, and cover with aluminum foil. Place on the cool side of your grill, close the lid and cook for 30 to 40 minutes, or until soft. Serve immediately on individual plates.

GRILLED PB'N'B
SANDWICHES
WITH WHISKY CREAM SAUCE

One summer, I was preparing to make this dish on TV to illustrate how to make grilled desserts. I wanted to skip a step, so I suggested that people could just buy bakery-made banana bread instead. After the segment aired on TV, it was hard to find a store that had any banana bread on hand—everyone was sold out because everyone was making this dish! To make this dish truly your own, use your favourite homemade banana-bread recipe.

1 small can sweetened condensed milk
2 to 3 Tbsp spiced whisky or dark rum
1 loaf banana bread
3 to 4 Tbsp smooth or crunchy peanut butter
1 banana, sliced

Pour the condensed milk into a small saucepan and warm slowly on low heat. Once warmed, remove the pan from the heat and add the whisky (or rum). Mix well and return to the heat to keep warm.

Prepare your grill for direct grilling, low to medium heat. Cut the loaf of banana bread into ½-inch slices. Smear peanut butter on one side of a slice, and then top with bananas and another slice of banana bread. (You will have 6 to 8 sandwiches depending on the size of the loaf.) Place the sandwiches on the grill and cook until warmed through, turning them once. Don't worry if you don't get grill marks, even though it adds to the cool factor of this dish. Remove from the heat. If you want smaller portions, cut the sandwiches in half.

To serve, arrange 1 whole or 2 half sandwiches on individual plates. Drizzle liberally with the warm whisky cream sauce, and enjoy!

GRILLED "CINNAMON TOAST"
WITH FRESH FRUIT PAN SAUCE

SERVES 6 TO 10

This is the easiest dessert I have ever made. It sounds dramatic but its simplicity is a cook's secret. Top with ice cream or whipped cream and enjoy!

¼ cup butter

¾ cup lightly packed brown sugar

3 to 4 cups fresh or frozen blackberries, blueberries, raspberries or a mix

1 Tbsp ground cinnamon

¼ cup white sugar

1 storebought angel food cake, cut into wedges

Melt the butter and brown sugar in a sauté pan on low to medium heat. Add the berries and bring to a boil. Reduce the heat to low, and simmer until the sauce becomes thick, 10 to 15 minutes. To check, draw a rubber scraper across the pan. If the liquid fills in quickly behind the scraper, it's runny. If it takes a moment to fill in, then it's starting to thicken. Keep the sauce warm while you prepare the "toast."

Prepare your grill for direct cooking, medium heat. In a small bowl, mix together the cinnamon and white sugar. Sprinkle the mixture over both sides of the angel food cake wedges. Place the cake on the grill, and toast the wedges to give them a little bit of colour. Keep a close eye on the cake as this will not take long, often just a minute or so. Transfer the toasted cake to individual plates.

Ladle some of the berries and syrup over the cake and serve.

I had been creating and selling House of Q sauces for a few years, but as people were sampling our products, one comment kept coming up: "Do you have a spicy sauce?" We didn't, which motivated me to craft a great-tasting, spicy sauce with character. I wanted to use what I had learned from wine tasting to allow people to experience different flavours on the palate as the sauce is eaten. First, I wanted to focus on sweetness followed by fragrant spices, such as nutmeg and cinnamon, and finally by spicy heat.

The sugars came together nicely and provided a great glossy coating in the sauce. Although I changed up the fragrant spices a bit through the testing process, ultimately I was really close to what I had been visualizing for the sauce. The challenge, however, was finding the right finishing heat. I tried chipotle peppers, jalapeños, habaneros, black pepper and even liquid capsicum (which is dangerous to play with!). All of them were too hot, or not hot enough, or in many instances, the flavours "mashed" together so there was no discernible separation between them. Although it was interesting to see how each spice I added to the recipe had different results, I wasn't getting a great-tasting sauce.

Finally, after many trial batches, I went back to simply using cayenne pepper. Much to my surprise, that single spice allowed the sauce to be hot without compromising the sweetness or the fragrant middle tones. Yum!

JACK DANIEL'S MAPLE PECAN PIE CINNAMON BUN
BREAD PUDDING

For a competitive BBQ cook, one of the most prestigious events to be invited to is the Jack Daniel's World Championship Invitational Barbecue. Many teams compete for years and win regional contests; however, they still never get invited to cook at the "Jack." House of Q was invited to this event for the first time in 2009, and our teammate Angie Quaale crafted this awesome dessert recipe. She had packed special ceramic presentation bowls in her luggage. When she arrived in Lynchburg, Tennessee, we discovered that all of the dishes were cracked or broken. Angie was discouraged, but she found some replacements, and House of Q went on to a fifth-place finish in the Best Dessert category. Needless to say, we celebrated like we were superheroes! Congratulations, Angie. What a dish! Serve warm with whipped cream and, of course, a side of sipping whiskey.

BREAD PUDDING

2 large eggs

5 egg yolks

2 cups half-and-half cream

1½ cups lightly packed brown sugar

2 Tbsp Jack Daniel's whiskey

6 to 8 storebought cinnamon buns,
    day old, roughly chopped

PECAN PIE TOPPING

2 Tbsp butter, melted

2 large eggs, room temperature

1½ cups lightly packed brown sugar

¼ cup maple syrup

1 Tbsp Jack Daniel's whiskey

1½ cup pecans, roughly chopped

BREAD PUDDING Prepare your grill for indirect cooking on medium heat. Have ready a 9- × 13-inch heatproof baking dish.

In a medium bowl, whisk together the whole eggs, egg yolks, cream, brown sugar and whiskey.

Cut or tear the cinnamon buns into rough chunks, and arrange them in a single layer in the bottom of the baking dish. Pour the custard mixture over the cinnamon buns, and allow them to soak for 10 minutes, pressing them down gently to ensure the bread absorbs the moisture. Once the bread has soaked up the custard, allow it to puff back up.

PECAN PIE TOPPING In a medium bowl, whisk together the butter, eggs, brown sugar, maple syrup and whiskey until well blended. Fold in the pecans.

FINISH PUDDING Pour the pecan pie mixture over the bread pudding; it might look a little sloppy but the buns will soak it all up.

Place the baking dish in a roasting pan and loosely cover with aluminum foil, leaving plenty of room for the pudding to expand. Poke a few holes in the foil to allow steam to escape, and then close the lid and grill-roast the pudding for 30 to 45 minutes. Remove the foil and cook for another 30 minutes, or until the pudding is golden brown, the topping has caramelized and the custard is set. Remove from the grill and allow to cool slightly. To serve, scoop out individual portions.

BACON
BAKLAVA

In Greece and the Middle East, baklava is as common a dessert as ice cream is in our country. This is my interpretation of this layered pastry, made with bacon instead of the classic pistachio nut filling.

Butter, for greasing the pan
¾ cup white sugar
¾ cup honey
1 cup water
1 Tbsp lemon juice
2 cups fried-until-crisp, cooled and chopped bacon (about 1½ lbs raw bacon)
1 cup lightly packed brown sugar
½ tsp ground cinnamon
1 lb frozen phyllo sheets, thawed
1 cup butter, melted

Prepare your grill for indirect cooking or smoking on medium heat. Grease a 9- × 13-inch baking pan with butter.

In a small saucepan, combine the white sugar, honey, water and lemon juice. Bring to a boil on low to medium heat, and cook this syrup for about 20 minutes, stirring occasionally, until syrupy. Allow the syrup to cool to room temperature.

In a small bowl, combine the bacon, brown sugar and cinnamon until well mixed.

Unwrap the phyllo pastry and cover the sheets with a damp dish towel to keep them from drying out. Place the melted butter in a small bowl. Using a pastry brush and working quickly, place 1 sheet of phyllo in the baking pan, and brush it liberally with butter. Sprinkle the bacon mixture over the pastry and then add another layer of pastry. Repeat the layering of pastry, brushing with butter and sprinkling with bacon until you have used all but one of the phyllo sheets. Set the last sheet on top and brush with the remaining butter.

Using a very sharp knife, cut the baklava into 2-inch squares or if you want a more traditional shape, cut into diamonds. Set the baking pan on the cool side of your grill, close the lid and bake or smoke until crisp and brown, 30 to 35 minutes. Remove from the heat. Pour the syrup mixture over the baklava and allow to cool to room temperature. Serve family-style, and watch as your guests lick the tasty syrup from their fingers.

GRILLED PUMPKIN-STUFFED
FRENCH TOAST

SERVES 6 TO 8

You can cook a lot of things on the grill, including brunch or breakfast dishes. We made this dish for Christmas morning breakfast one year, and it has been a signature dish ever since. This dish is also perfect for dessert! Serve it with fresh or grilled fruit, maple syrup or your favourite topping for French toast. I like it with the pan sauce from the Grilled "Cinnamon Toast" with Fresh Fruit Pan Sauce (page 150).

2 cups ricotta cheese
1 small can pumpkin purée
1 to 2 tsp ground ginger
1 to 2 tsp ground cinnamon
1 tsp ground allspice
9 eggs
1 cup half-and-half cream
2 cups white sugar
1 tsp sea salt or kosher salt
2 loaves of French bread
Vegetable oil or butter, for greasing
Maple syrup

In a large bowl, combine the ricotta and pumpkin purée until well mixed. Stir in the ginger, cinnamon and allspice. Cover and refrigerate until needed.

To make the custard, break the eggs into a large bowl. Add the cream, sugar and salt and whisk until well mixed.

Cut and discard the crust from one end of the bread. Then move the knife over a ½ inch and cut most—but not all—of the way through the bread. Move the knife over another ½ inch and, this time, slice all the way through the bread. You will have a "2-piece" slice of bread that is attached on the bottom. Continue cutting "2-piece" slices from both loaves. (You should have 8 to 12 of them.) Fill each pocket with 1 to 2 tablespoons of the pumpkin filling and set aside.

Prepare your grill for direct cooking, low to medium heat. Place a sheet of aluminum foil on top of the grate, and lightly spray it with vegetable oil or melt some butter on top. Dip a filled bread pocket in the custard, turn it over to coat it well and then place it on the foil. Repeat with the remaining bread pockets. Close the lid and cook the French toast, in batches if necessary, turning them once until the egg custard has set and is no longer runny, 5 to 10 minutes per side. Once the egg custard has set, place each French toast directly on the grates to create some grill marks and colour.

To serve, load the French toast onto a serving platter and pass it around. Serve warm with your favourite toppings.

BRINES, RUBS, SAUCES AND SPREADS

THERE ARE A NUMBER OF WAYS TO PREPARE MEATS AND FOODS TO ENHANCE, CONTRAST OR COMPLEMENT THEIR NATURAL FLAVOUR. I AM A STRONG PROPONENT OF USING BRINES FOR MEATS, RUBS FOR SEASONING AND, WELL, SAUCES AND DIPS TO ADD ANOTHER LAYER OF FLAVOUR.

BASE
BRINE

This brine recipe contains a good ratio of salt and sugar to water, and time and again, I've found that this well-seasoned brine produces a perfectly flavoured meat. If you are brining something small, cut the recipe by half or more—but be sure to maintain the same ratio. Add the meat to the brine only once it's cool. And once you've added the meat to the brine, plan on leaving it immersed for one hour per pound of meat before you remove it.

16 cups water (1 gallon)
1 cup sea salt or kosher salt
1 cup lightly packed brown sugar
6 to 8 cups ice (or more)

Place the water in a large stockpot, cooler or food-safe plastic bucket. Add the salt and brown sugar and stir until dissolved. Add ice to cool it down.

CIDER
BRINE

Experiment with apple, peach or your favourite fresh non-alcoholic cider. This brine is excellent with pork or chicken.

4 cups water
⅓ to ½ cup kosher salt
4 cups apple cider or apple juice
3 to 5 cups ice (or more)

Place the water in a stockpot, cooler or food-safe plastic bucket. Add the salt and stir until dissolved. Add the cider and ice to cool it down.

Cooking for the most part, especially barbecue, is all about creating really appealing flavours. A lesson I learned as a competitive BBQ cook is that you can layer flavours at different points during the cooking process to build a total food experience. One popular technique that I like to use is brining, which is sometimes confused with marinating (page 104).

Brining is all about the science of pressure. Imagine that you've just jumped into a swimming pool and sunk to the bottom. With all the increased water pressure, your head might feel like it is going to implode. That is the same principle that explains how brining works. A brine is a basic solution, usually salt and water, that is often flavoured with herbs, spices and other seasonings. By immersing meats in this seasoned liquid, the increased pressure forces the seasonings and the liquid deep into the meat, thereby making it more moist, more flavourful and a bit more forgiving to being overcooked. A brine is all about adding flavour to the inside, whereas a marinade is all about flavouring the outside of the meat.

There are three key rules to keep in mind when working with brines:

1. ADD WHATEVER SEASONINGS YOU LIKE, BUT DISSOLVE THEM IN WATER FIRST. Steeping solid ingredients in warm or even hot water to extract their flavour is the best way to flavour your brine. Common additions beyond salt and sugar are garlic, cloves, cinnamon, bay leaves, peppercorns and other whole spices. Just remember to cool the steeped mixture before you finish the rest of the brine.

2. KEEP BRINES COLD, REALLY COLD. By keeping the temperature below 40°F, you minimize the possibility of bacterial growth and you increase the pressure in the brine. Double-check the temperature of your fridge with a thermometer if you are not sure whether it's cold enough—and use plenty of ice in the brine.

3. BRINE MEATS FOR ONE HOUR PER POUND OF MEAT. So, if you are brining a four-pound roasting chicken, plan on four hours. Brine a 12-pound turkey for 12 or more hours. If you are brining a bunch of shrimp, an hour or two is fine (they're tiny!).

It is common to hear that people will continue to use a brining technique once they have tried it. The Thanksgiving turkey is more moist, the Saturday-night chicken is juicier and the Tuesday-night pork chops simply taste fantastic!

ALL ABOUT
BRINES

HONEY
BRINE

This brine provides an awesome flavour for turkey or chicken. For even more flavour, steep mulling spice in this brine.

16 cups cold water (1 gallon)
2 to 8 Tbsp mulled wine spice (optional)
1 cup sea salt or kosher salt
1 cup honey
6 to 8 cups ice (or more)

If you're using the mulling spice, in a medium saucepan, combine 2 to 4 cups of water and the spice. Bring the mixture to a boil, reduce the heat to low and allow it to steep until the flavours have infused into the water. Allow the mixture to cool to room temperature.

Pour the infusion into a large stockpot, cooler or food-safe plastic bucket. Add the remaining water, salt and honey and stir until dissolved. Add ice to cool it down.

MAPLE
BRINE

This is a great brine for pork or poultry or for wowing your guests with a smoked turkey.

16 cups cold water (1 gallon)
1 cup sea salt or kosher salt
1 cup maple syrup
6 to 8 cups ice (or more)

Place the water in a large stockpot, cooler or food-safe plastic bucket. Add the salt and maple syrup and stir until dissolved. Add ice to cool it down.

BASIC
BBQ RUB

Every good grill cook has his or her own special rub, a mixture of spices to coat and season foods. Most rubs are a balanced blend of salty, sweet and fragrant ingredients. This recipe is a base to which you can add whatever unique touches you want, such as basil, oregano, rosemary, ginger, cinnamon, nutmeg, cayenne, other kinds of paprika and chili powder and so on. Just add small amounts, such as a teaspoon, at a time so you avoid any overdominant flavour. Sprinkle this rub on your choice of meat, seafood or vegetables before cooking them.

½ cup white sugar

½ cup lightly packed brown sugar

⅓ cup seasoned salt

¼ cup sea salt or kosher salt

⅓ cup coarsely ground black pepper

⅓ cup granulated garlic

⅓ cup chili powder

⅓ cup paprika, sweet or spicy or even smoky

¼ cup onion powder

¼ cup celery powder

In a medium bowl, combine the sugars, salts and all of the spices and mix well. Sift through a colander to evenly mix the spices, if you like. Will keep in an airtight container for months.

BIG
BEEF RUB

MAKES 2¼ CUPS

Whenever I'm doing a prime rib roast or a big chunk of beef, I like to keep the crust simple yet complementary. This is my go-to beef rub. Coat your beef, such as tri-tip, prime rib or even steaks, well and cook as planned.

1 cup seasoned salt
½ cup granulated garlic
½ cup black pepper
¼ cup minced fresh or dried rosemary

In a medium bowl, combine all of the ingredients and mix well. Will keep in a resealable plastic bag or an airtight container for months.

CHICKEN RUB

MAKES 2½ CUPS

This rub has an initial salty flavour followed by a nice balance of heat and fragrance.

1 cup white sugar
¾ cup seasoning salt
3 Tbsp black pepper
3 Tbsp chili powder
3 Tbsp paprika
2 Tbsp celery powder
2 Tbsp granulated garlic
2 Tbsp onion powder
1 Tbsp ground cinnamon
1 Tbsp ground allspice

In a medium bowl, combine all of the ingredients and mix well. Sift through a colander to evenly blend the spices, if you like. Will keep in an airtight container for months.

PORK CRUST

MAKES ⅓ CUP

Our House of Q House Rub is designed to be easily adapted by backyard cooks. This pork crust is an example of how to take a commercial product and make your own unique rub just by adding a few ingredients. Sprinkle this rub on pork loin roasts or chops before smoking them.

3 to 4 Tbsp House of Q House Rub or
    Basic BBQ Rub (page 164)
1 Tbsp ground cumin
1 tsp cayenne pepper

In a medium bowl, combine the rub, cumin and cayenne pepper and mix well. Will keep in an airtight container for months.

PORK RIB RUB

MAKES 3 CUPS

I like this rub on ribs and, if I recall correctly, we used to use this one in competition for a few years.

1 cup lightly packed brown sugar
1 cup seasoned salt
½ cup paprika
3 Tbsp chili powder
2 Tbsp dry mustard
1 Tbsp onion powder
1 Tbsp celery powder
1 Tbsp black pepper

In a medium bowl, combine the brown sugar, salt and spices and mix well. Sift through a colander to evenly mix the spices, if you like. Will keep in an airtight container for months.

ORANGE-GINGER
BARBECUE SAUCE

MAKES 3 TO 4 CUPS

This sauce is great with pork and chicken. It's easy to make too!

2 Tbsp olive oil

1 small onion, grated

3 cloves garlic, minced

One 3-inch piece fresh ginger, peeled and grated

1½ cans tomato paste

4 cups orange juice

3 whole star anise

2 tsp ground cumin

1 Tbsp sea salt or kosher salt

1 Tbsp black pepper

3 Tbsp plain white vinegar

Heat a sauté pan on medium heat. Add the olive oil, onions, garlic and ginger, and sauté until the onions are soft and the mixture is fragrant, about 5 minutes. Whisk in the tomato paste and orange juice until well combined, and then stir in the remaining ingredients. Simmer uncovered for 15 to 20 minutes, stirring every few minutes, until the sauce thickens and coats the back of a spoon. Will keep refrigerated in an airtight container for 3 weeks.

WHITE
BARBECUE SAUCE

MAKES 2 CUPS

This recipe, also known as Smoked Onion and Garlic Barbecue Sauce, started with a couple of heads of garlic and a few onions that we threw into the smoker when we had some extra space. Traditionally, this sauce is used as a glaze for chicken in Alabama, and it is absolutely fantastic as a condiment for your burgers.

1 head of garlic

1 onion

Olive oil

2 tsp sea salt or kosher salt

2 tsp black pepper

1 cup mayonnaise

2 Tbsp apple cider vinegar

2 Tbsp lemon juice

1 tsp cayenne pepper

Prepare your grill for smoking, low heat. Using a sharp knife, cut off and discard the pointed top of the garlic head and the outer layer of the onion. Place the onion and garlic on a sheet of aluminum foil, gathering it around the base of the vegetables so they cannot roll around. Leave the tops exposed, drizzle with olive oil, season with salt and pepper, and then place them on the cool side of your grill. Cook for about 45 minutes, until soft and cooked through.

Squeeze the garlic and onion flesh into a food processor and discard the peel. Add the mayonnaise, cider vinegar, lemon juice and cayenne pepper, pulse until chopped and then process until smooth. Season to taste with more salt or pepper. Will keep refrigerated in an airtight container for 4 to 6 months.

APPLE BUTTER
ONIONS

Use these caramelized onions on burgers or any pork dish, or even as an appetizer on crackers and cheese. You can use another barbecue sauce, but then these won't be Apple Butter Onions!

3 to 4 Tbsp butter
1 to 2 sweet onions, sliced
½ to 1 cup House of Q Apple Butter BBQ Sauce

Melt the butter in a sauté pan on low to medium heat. Add the onions and sauté until soft but not browned, about 20 minutes. Add the BBQ sauce and simmer, uncovered, for another 30 to 45 minutes or until it has the consistency of a thick chutney. Will keep refrigerated in an airtight container for up to 2 months.

GRILLED
TOMATO SALSA

Storebought salsa often simply doesn't seem to have enough flavour, especially once you've made your own. It's easy too!

8 medium tomatoes
Olive oil
2 jalapeño peppers, seeded and membranes removed
1 yellow onion
Juice of ½ lime
Kosher salt
Chopped fresh cilantro, to taste

Prepare your grill for direct cooking, medium-high heat. Rinse the tomatoes, brush them with olive oil and place 4 of them on the cool side of the grill. Cook, turning them frequently, until the tomatoes are charred on the outside but still firm on the inside. Remove them from the grill and allow the tomatoes to cool.

Using a sharp knife, chop the remaining tomatoes in half, remove and discard the seeds and dice the flesh in ¼-inch pieces. Place the diced tomatoes in a large bowl. Finely dice the jalapeño peppers and onion, and add them to the bowl and mix gently. Dice the charred tomatoes and add them to the mix. Pour in the lime juice, season with salt and stir in the cilantro.

Serve at room temperature or chill until ready to serve. Will keep refrigerated in an airtight container for a couple of days.

SMOKED
SQUASH SPREAD

This spread can turn a burger that's just okay into a great one! It is also delicious served with crackers or sliced bread as an appetizer.

1 butternut squash, about ¾ to 1 lb
Olive oil, for drizzling
Salt and black pepper
½ to 1 cup cream cheese
½ to 1 tsp ground turmeric

Prepare your grill for indirect cooking, medium heat. Cut a large sheet of aluminum foil.

Rinse the squash and carefully cut it in half lengthwise. Scoop out and discard the seeds. Place the squash, flesh side up, on a sheet of foil. Drizzle both halves with olive oil, and season with salt and pepper. Wrap up the squash in the foil, set it on the grate, close the lid and roast for 45 to 60 minutes, or until a knife slides easily into the squash. Remove the squash from the grill and allow it to cool. Unwrap the squash and discard the foil.

Using a spoon, scoop the flesh into a food processor, discarding any burned or stringy bits that might not be too tasty. Add the cream cheese and turmeric and blend until smooth. If the dip becomes too runny, add more cream cheese. Season to taste with salt and pepper. Transfer the spread to a bowl and refrigerate until ready to serve.

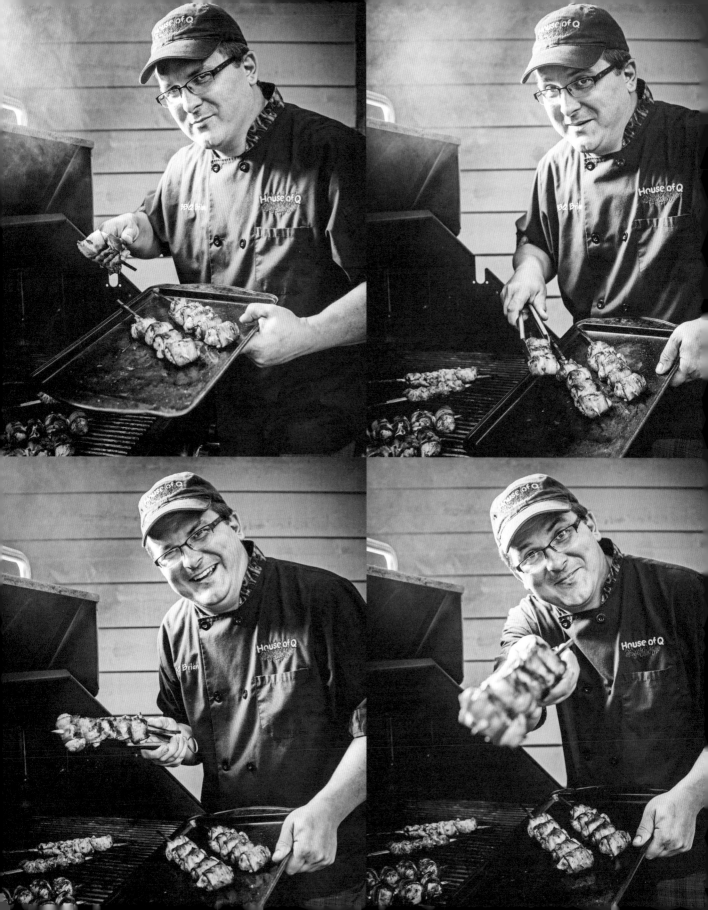

ACKNOWLEDGEMENTS

In my mind, I can picture that I am onstage at an awards ceremony like the Academy Awards and that I've just won the Best Actor category and have an opportunity to acknowledge a few people. I am not sure if I am that actor; however, I can at least imagine how stars feel as they acknowledge the people who have helped get them to where they are, hoping not to miss someone or run out of time before the microphone shuts off.

My wife, Corinne, is the love of my life, my business partner and my competition cookmate. She is also the mother of my daughter, Kassandra. These two are the first in line to taste, advise, provide feedback and tell me sincerely if whatever I am cooking is good or not so good. For that and for your never-ending support, thank you.

Ingrid Kraus, Corinne's sister, is always available to help, regardless of the task. She samples at events, delivers BBQ sauce, sits with Kass when Corinne and I are not around. Thank you.

Our families have been very supportive, from simply listening to what's going on to helping with setting up or tearing down at events. A big thank you to our parents, Noelle and Al Misko and Fred and Lottie Kraus, and to my siblings, Kelly, Val and Ken. You always seem to be there when needed.

To Glenn Erho, I'd like to say thank you for playing with me. Our adult "sandbox time," which has involved cooking, travelling, talking, competing and discovering, has laid the foundation for where I am today.

Thank you to Karen Olenik for providing a kitchen and words of encouragement, along with quite possibly the world's largest cookbook collection to look through.

To Angie Quaale, I say thank you for seeing the talent I didn't quite see in myself yet. You have encouraged me to grow.

I can visualize the exact moment when Ron Shewchuk said, "Just do it and you will never look back." Though I didn't and couldn't have known it at the time, I haven't. Thank you, Ron, for being the role model that I have tried to follow.

Thank you to Steve Darling for being a big supporter and promoter of House of Q. You are quite possibly the biggest fan of Apple Butter BBQ Sauce ever! I love it!

I'd like to also thank Weber, Primo Ceramic Grills, Yoder Smokers and Crown Verity for providing some of the best gear a person could ever want.

And lastly, a big thank you to the store owners who have willingly brought our products into their businesses and the thousands of people who love our sauces. Thank you. You have allowed me to experience in a whole new and unimaginable way the simple lesson that Mom taught me about sharing. Your enthusiasm for our products and the lessons I share is very touching and rewarding. Thank you!

METRIC
CONVERSION CHARTS

WEIGHT

IMPERIAL OR U.S.	METRIC
1 oz	30 g
2 oz	60 g
3 oz	90 g
4 oz	125 g
5 oz	150 g
6 oz	175 g
7 oz	200 g
8 oz (½ lb)	250 g
9 oz	270 g
12 oz	375 g
1 lb (16 oz)	500 g
2 lbs	1 kg
3 lbs	1.5 kg
5 lbs	2.3 kg
8 lbs	3.5 kg
10 lbs	4.5 kg
12 lbs	5.5 kg
14 lbs	6.4 kg

VOLUME

IMPERIAL OR U.S.	METRIC
¼ tsp	1 mL
½ tsp	2.5 mL
1 tsp	5 mL
1 Tbsp	15 mL
1½ Tbsp	23 mL
2 Tbsp	30 mL
¼ cup	60 mL
⅓ cup	80 mL
6 Tbsp	90 mL
½ cup	125 mL
⅔ cup	160 mL
¾ cup	185 mL
1 cup	250 mL
1¼ cups	310 mL
1½ cups	375 mL
1¾ cups	435 mL
2 cups	500 mL
2¼ cups	560 mL
2½ cups	625 mL
2¾ cups	685 mL
3 cups	750 mL
4 cups	1 L
5 cups	1.25 L
6 cups	1.5 L
8 cups	2 L
16 cups (1 gallon)	4 L

LENGTH

IMPERIAL OR U.S.	METRIC
¼ inch	6 mm
⅜ inch	10 mm
½ inch	12 mm
¾ inch	2 cm
1 inch	2.5 cm
1¼ inches	3 cm
1½ inches	3.5 cm
2 inches	5 cm
3 inches	7.5 cm
4 inches	10 cm
5 inches	12.5 cm
6 inches	15 cm
7 inches	18 cm
8 inches	20 cm
9 inches	23 cm
10 inches	25 cm
12 inches	30 cm
13 inches	33 cm
14 inches	35 cm
16 inches	40 cm

TEMPERATURE

IMPERIAL OR U.S.	METRIC
110°F	43°C
115°F	46°C
120°F	49°C
125°F	52°C
130°F	54°C
135°F	57°C
140°F	60°C
145°F	63°C
150°F	66°C
155°F	68°C
160°F	71°C
165°F	74°C
170°F	77°C
175°F	79°C
180°F	82°C
185°F	85°C
190°F	88°C
195°F	91°C
200°F	93°C
225°F	107°C
250°F	121°C
275°F	135°C
300°F	149°C
325°F	163°C
350°F	177°C
375°F	191°C
400°F	204°C
425°F	218°C
450°F	232°C

INDEX

in grilled tomato
salsa, 168
jalapeño 'n' cheese
cornbread waffle
burgers, 38–40, 39
in Thai-style shrimp-
stuffed chicken
breast, 83
Jarlsberg
in cheese-stuffed bacon-
wrapped hot dogs, 35
in grilled asparagus
tart, 136

L
lemons and lemon juice
in bacon baklava, 154
in grilled whole salmon
with yoghurt dill
sauce, 99
lemon and herb-crusted
chicken, 80
in shrimp tacos, 94
in top secret chicken
brine, 119
in white barbecue
sauce, 167
lettuce wraps, chicken
and prawn, 20
limes and lime juice
chili-lime sauce, 109
in citrus chicken with
raspberry barbecue
sauce, 76
in grilled corn, black bean
and peach salad, 138
in grilled tomato salad,
168
in grilled whole salmon
with yoghurt dill
sauce, 99
in House of Q fish and
chips, 101
in shrimp tacos, 94

M
mac 'n' cheese, 142, 143
mango, in Thai-style
shrimp-stuffed
chicken breast, 83
maple syrup

in Big Al's planked
halibut, 106
in cedar-planked
Brie with cranberry
chutney, 18
maple and mustard pork
tenderloins, 53
maple brine, 163
maple salmon, 98
in pecan pie topping, 153
in smoked ribs, 50
mayo, chipotle, 101
mayonnaise
in Big Al's planked
halibut, 106
in Brussels sprout
coleslaw, 139
chipotle mayo, 100, 101
in Cori's potato salad, 130
in sesame dressing, 131
in Southern slaw, 138
in white barbecue
sauce, 167
meatloaf. *See also* burgers;
sausages
cranked-up meatloaf,
48, 49
dinosaur eggs, 24, 25
Merlot sauce, cherry, with,
grilled duck breasts, 91
Monterey Jack
in cheese-stuffed
bacon-wrapped
hot dogs, 35
in cranked-up
meatloaf, 49
in grilled black bean and
mushroom burritos, 21
in mac 'n' cheese
(jalapeño Jack), 143
moo and oink balls of
wonderment, 22
mozzarella, in cheese-
stuffed bacon-wrapped
hot dogs, 35
mushroom and black bean
burritos, grilled, 21
mustard. *See also* House of Q
Slow Smoke Gold
BBQ Sauce and Slather
grill-roasted Brussels

sprouts with warm
mustard and bacon
vinaigrette, 135
maple and mustard
pork tenderloins, 53
mustard mop, 54
in pork rib rub, 166

N
no-fail smoked chicken
wings, 29
nori wraps, barbecued
chicken in, 78–79

O
onions
apple butter onions,
53, 168
in Brian's cornbread, 140
in Brussels sprout
coleslaw, 139
in grilled tomato
salsa, 168
in shaved fennel and
onion salad, 139
smoked onion and garlic
creamed orzo, 141
in white barbecue
sauce, 167
orange-ginger barbecue
sauce, 167
orange juice
in citrus chicken with
raspberry barbecue
sauce, 76
in grilled halibut, 101
in orange-ginger
barbecue sauce, 167
in raspberry barbecue
sauce, 76
in rhubarb-marinated
pork tenderloins with
Jack Daniel's apples, 57
orzo, smoked onion and
garlic creamed, 141
oysters à la House of Q,
grilled, 105

P
Parmesan, in
mac 'n' cheese, 143

pastries
bacon baklava, 154, 155
grilled asparagus tart, 136
peach, grilled corn and
black bean and salad, 138
peanut butter, in grilled
PB 'n' B sandwiches with
whisky cream sauce, 149
pecan pie topping, 153
pepper-crusted beef sirloin
with Cambozola cheese,
60, 61
phyllo sheets, for bacon
baklava, 154
planked crab-stuffed
peppers, 102, 103
pork. *See also* bacon
bacon bites, 26, 27
beer-brined pork
chops, 46
in breakfast sausage
burgers, 38
championship slow-
smoked ribs, 114–116,
115
cheese-stuffed bacon-
wrapped hot dogs,
34, 35
in cranked-up meatloaf,
49
grilled pork tenderloins,
53
in handmade Italian
sausage burgers, 36
maple and mustard
pork tenderloins, 53
prosciutto and basil–
wrapped prawns,
108, 109
pulled pork, 126–127
rhubarb-marinated pork
tenderloins with Jack
Daniel's apples, 57
smoked ribs, 50, 51
spinach-stuffed pork
chops, 54, 55
pork rubs
pork crust, 166
pork rib rub, 166
simple pork rub,
46

HOUSE OF Q

House of Q is an award-winning competition-BBQ team based in Surrey, B.C. Since starting to cook competitively in 2005, the team has accumulated awards locally and across North America. House of Q attended the Jack Daniel's World Championship Invitational Barbecue in Lynchburg, Tennessee, in 2009 and 2014 and twice has gone to the Best of the Best Competition at the National BBQ Festival in Douglas, Georgia. Twice the team has attended the American Royal World Series of Barbecue Invitational Contest in Kansas City, Missouri, in 2012 and 2014. In 2010 and 2012, House of Q was honoured as the Team of the Year for British Columbia, and it was honoured as the Canadian BBQ Society Team of the Year for 2014. BBQ Brian was invited as a guest chef at the Vancouver 2010 Winter Olympics.

House of Q launched its BBQ sauce and spice line in 2007, and its signature Apple Butter BBQ Sauce has been declared the number one barbecue sauce in Alberta twice at the BBQ on the Bow barbecue championships and the third-best barbecue sauce in North America at the National BBQ Festival in Douglas, Georgia. In 2012 and 2013, the Slow Smoke Gold BBQ Sauce and Slather was awarded second-best sauce at the American Royal World Series of Barbecue in Kansas City. House of Q products have a loyal following and are bestsellers at specialty retailers across Canada.

BBQ Brian shares his know-how through regular interviews and cooking demonstrations on TV, in newspapers and in magazines. Thousands have seen his "BBQ Tips" on Global BC's *Morning News,* at a trade show cooking demonstration or at cooking classes across western Canada. Find out more about House of Q at houseofq.com.